The Autism Diaries

This is a nonfiction biographical narrative compilation, and all obtained information is herein property of the author. Certain names and details were changed to protect the identity of the participating interviewees and their families.

This book was created in honor of all the strong mothers and other women who assume the role of raising children with autism spectrum disorder. You are amazing stewards in this journey! You possess an extraordinary ability to find the beauty and witness the miracles beyond the struggles.

The Autism Diaries

Raising Children with Autism Through Mothers' Eyes

Stephanie Ortega-Ramirez, MS, PPS

Contents

DISCLAIMER

This book is based on interviews conducted with real mothers of children with autism spectrum disorder and other special needs. These women consented to sharing all or part of their stories, so that other parents can learn from their experiences in raising differently-abled children. Some names were changed to respect the privacy of those who requested to do so. This book contains opinions, theories, and conclusions drawn from each personal experience. This book does not claim to provide expert medical, therapeutic, or legal advice. The purpose of this book is for readers to get a real glimpse at raising children with autism, as experienced by mothers.

The Autism Diaries

Real Stories From Real Autism Mothers

If you're looking at this book, chances are you're an autism mother, grandmother, or you know someone with autism spectrum disorder (ASD). Well, I'm glad you've made the decision to read this book! Throughout the pages, you will meet nine different women. All are mothers of children with autism and other special needs. You will get a glimpse into their lives with all the challenges and triumphs they've experienced, and have so graciously shared. There is no better way to understand autism, than by living it, and these stories will bring you pretty close to that.

This book will take you through several tours of autism, and some of the variations of the disorder that exist, from first-hand accounts. Through these stories you will learn helpful tips in navigating a world with autism, a better understanding of the condition, and how to become a strong advocate.

It is my hope that you gain insight from the experiences shared, by these extraordinary mothers.

About Your Author

Autism is something near and dear to my heart. I was introduced to it formally over a decade ago, when my own son was diagnosed at almost three years old. My son has been my greatest teacher. He is severely affected by autism. His condition makes it difficult for him to communicate, make friends or connect with others, and basically live a "normal" life. My world is shaped around my son's needs. I can definitely say that this life is not easy, but I wouldn't trade it for the world! Through my own journey in raising a family with special needs, I have found a unique purpose. I have experienced immense pain and overwhelming joy. In our lives surrounding autism, I have witnessed many miracles in my son, which I may have otherwise taken for granted.

Before autism came into my life, I was a graduate student with big plans. All of that changed when my son was diagnosed. I took the skills I learned, and fought for finding the right professionals and therapies, to provide him the support he needed. I also recognized that there was no manual for this kind of life. After facing all the obstacles we had to go through to obtain services and other supports, I knew I had gained a wealth of knowledge. I wanted to share with other parents in similar situations. With the help of two other mothers, we founded a nonprofit organization called, Fresno Autism Network (FAN). FAN was established to provide supportive services to families of children with autism, in the Central Valley.

Being the CEO of FAN, has brought me a great deal of joy and satisfaction. There's nothing like the feeling of being able to help other families, through their struggles, and see their children thrive with the right supports in place. Who would've thought that one little boy's life, would touch so many people's lives? It still amazes me today!

My family is a bit seasoned in living with autism, but we are still young in the journey. It has been a complete blessing to learn from other parents, who have been further down the path that we're on. Those parents have offered helpful tips and suggestions, based on what they've tried with their own children at difficult times along the way. I am forever grateful to all of the people who have been instrumental in our navigation through a life with autism.

Just as I continue to learn and grow in the new seasons of my own story in raising a family with autism, I hope to provide all readers a bit of the same insight. I'm eager to know if there are any similar themes, processes, or experiences among the stories in this book, that readers can relate to. At the end of each chapter you will find a section called, *My Take*, which is where I'll explain the main points I took from each story.

The Process

Being in contact with hundreds of autism families over the last decade, I was afforded the opportunity to get to know some of them. I sent a message to several of the mothers, inquiring if they'd be interested in sharing their stories with me for this book. Over the last two years, I was able to connect with the mothers who's stories were included. I met with all but one of the ladies in person. After all the technical agreements and signatures were collected, I proceeded to interview each one of the mothers. I had a list of specific questions prepared. I honestly felt like a reporter at times!

Even though I had those questions ready, and the ladies can attest to this, the stories just unfolded with ease after the first few questions were answered. Every single story fascinated me. I can't explain how incredibly honored I felt, hearing all of them for the first time. It was a lengthy process, but worth every minute! I wanted to make sure to do justice to the narrative that was described to me by each one of the interviewees.

Grab Your Tissues

I want to again emphasize the significance of these first-hand accounts you are about to read. Remember, these are real experiences through the eyes of mothers. These are actual people with some raw quotes and vulnerable emotions, that will be revealed on the pages that follow. You might want to grab yourself some tissue, a paper and pen, and heck, maybe even some chocolate and a glass of wine!

CHAPTER 1

Unique Beauty

This is the story of Jodie Howard's journey with autism. Jodie and I met a little over six years ago. Our boys were attending the same autism therapy center at that time. I was referred to Jodie by several parents. I was trying to obtain intervention services for my own son and I needed help. Jodie was extremely helpful, and I was amazed at just how poised and put together she was. She was well versed in special education, and incredibly...fierce! It was an honor to have her as an advocate for my boy. I learned a great deal from Jodie, and we've since become better acquainted. We've worked on some small projects together for advocacy and parent empowerment, within our autism community.

Jodie is married, and a mother of two children. At the time of our interview, her son Bren was fourteen years old, and her daughter Sydney was almost twelve years old. Jodie was born and raised in Hawaii, and she met her husband on the mainland United States. After marriage the Howards happily started their family.

When Jodie was pregnant for the first time, the couple was over the moon to find out they were going to have a little boy. Jodie specifically remembers wondering about what her son's voice was going to sound like. It had fascinated her how boy's voices change as they become teenagers, then young men. As a little girl, Jodie envisioned herself growing up and becoming a mother of boys. She planned on having three boys, that would all be taller than her (I thought that was super cute). Jodie did end up a mom of *one* boy, who's definitely taller than her — she got that part right!

Bren's Arrival

Jodie's pregnancy with Bren, was relatively normal. She did, however, have a pretty rough delivery. Her kidneys had stopped functioning properly. Jodie had developed *preeclampsia*. Preeclampsia is a pregnancy complication characterized by high blood pressure (Mayo Clinic, 2020). The preeclampsia along with baby's size, resulted in an emergency situation during the pushing phase of labor. Bren was then born by *cesarian section*, or *c-section*. After the whirlwind of delivery subsided, everything calmed down. Mom and baby were healthy otherwise.

Then, similarly to my own experience, Jodie ended up back in the hospital with her newborn, due to him having *Jaundice*. Jaundice happens in infants when *bilirubin*, the yellowish substance in their blood, isn't broken down by the liver, causing yellowing of the skin (Medline Plus, 2020). Baby Bren had to spend a few days under the *bilirubin* lights. It's a treatment used to treat jaundice in infants. Finally, it was time for them to leave the hospital — again. The Howards were happy to go home with their new baby and start their life together.

Bren's Words

Baby Bren was growing beautifully. Jodie was excited to hear his first words! She remembers Bren's language starting to emerge when he was around seventeen months old. He was saying words like "mama", "dada", and other pretty basic baby words. Jodie's favorite word was, "banamanamanama". Yep, you read that right! Bren would say that when he wanted a banana. Jodie said, "It was so adorable, it seemed like it would trail on forever."

This made me think of the words I love to hear so much from my own little ones. I never like to overcorrect the cute utterances, because I know they'll eventually disappear. As Bren was the Howard's one and only child at that time, you could imagine how sweet those baby words sounded to their ears.

Something's Different With Bren

Like most toddlers, if he wanted something he couldn't get on his own, Bren would look to his mom or dad for help. He'd persist until he got the thing he wanted. Toddlers, can be pretty demanding.

On one particular day, Bren was standing in the kitchen of the apartment where they lived. He wanted a banana that was on the counter. Bren proceeded to do something completely out of character. Jodie explained how he simply pointed to the bananas, and then grunted. He didn't ask or try to say banana in that very cute way he usually did. He just grunted and pointed! This quickly caught Jodie's attention. She then realized it had been a while, since she had heard him say that adorable word. Jodie tried to coax it out of him. She encouraged Bren to say, "banamanamanama", "banana", or even to just make the, "b" sound, but he wouldn't! That cute run-on word was gone. Instead, Bren pointed, and grunted again! Jodie wondered how that word had suddenly disappeared.

Shouldn't it have started to become more developed, sounding more like banana, not reduced to a grunt?

Once Jodie and her husband noticed Bren's adorable word was gone, they started noticing other things that were different about their son. It became clear to them, he had not just lost his approximation of "banana", he had lost ALL — of his words. He stopped saying them! They also noticed that Bren often appeared to look past them, even when they were talking to him. "It was like the light in his eyes was extinguished," Jodie said. I felt the sadness in her recollection.

The Howards were now on a hunt to find out what was going on with their son. He wasn't speaking anymore! He wasn't engaged or interested in things like before. Jodie, being a practical and analytic minded person, turned to research articles for answers. Still, she found no answers. At least nothing that completely fit the description of her son's condition. There had to be something! Her niece is Autistic, so Jodie explored that possibility, but Bren's condition looked too different from his cousin's. Jodie dismissed the idea. Doctors kept telling the Howards that Bren was just delayed, and he'd catch up to his peers in time. Jodie was still very worried, so she continued to search for answers. Fortunately, being raised in a faith believing in an afterlife, Jodie didn't see the possibility of Bren having a disability, as completely devastating. If Bren in fact has a disability, "I know, I have the faith that in the next life, he won't have the disability, we'll be a family, we'll be together," Jodie remembered thinking.

The Diagnosis

After searching over a year for answers, Jodie came back to the idea that Bren might actually have autism. By that time, Jodie learned things about autism that she didn't know before. She learned that it could manifest differently among each individual with the disability. This explained why her niece's autism could look different than her own son's. Autism, was the only thing left that best described Bren's behaviors and disposition.

Jodie clearly remembers when Bren received his diagnosis. It was just shy of his third birthday. After being through countless assessments, the Howards went to *Exceptional Parents Unlimited (EPU)*, a nonprofit organization serving children with special needs and their families, in Fresno County.

The Howards were scheduled to meet with a doctor for Bren's assessment at EPU.

"Dr. S" is what she called him. He was one of the sweetest doctors Jodie had ever met. Dr. S observed Bren for less than 20 minutes. He then sat Jodie down, held her hands, and looked her right in the eyes. Jodie remembers him saying, "Im really sorry to tell you this, but your child *is* Autistic." Surprisingly, Jodie felt — immense relief. The Dr. must have been bracing her for a breakdown (a more common reaction), but the weight on her shoulders of searching for answers for what seemed like an eternity, was finally eased. Jodie admits that if they had received a diagnosis of autism without that year-and-a-half search for answers, her reaction might have been a little more emotional. In exploring countless possibilities to explain her son's condition, she had already worked through a lot of the hard emotions.

As mentioned before, Jodie wondered about what her son's voice was going to sound like, before he was born. Was it going to be deep? When would it change? Those were some of the thoughts she had about his voice. Ironically, however, Bren ended up being *nonverbal.*

Jodie has witnessed how some people take the diagnosis of autism much harder than she did. She has seen how sometimes, parents treat the child as if they've been replaced by some *different* child with a disability. She has NEVER— felt that way about Bren.

A mixture of being distracted by searching for answers, and having her faith, made coping with Bren's diagnosis easier for Jodie. "I have an amazing sister, who's daughter has autism… who walked me through everything," Jodie added. She says her sister cautioned her that life would be different with autism, but that didn't mean it was going to be bad. Her sister also assured Jodie that she'd find a "unique beauty" in her journey with autism.

Start of Services

After the the assessment process was completed at EPU, the Howards came across the *Central Valley Regional Center (CVRC)*, another agency that provides services to persons with disabilities. Like many special-needs families, to obtain services for their newly diagnosed child, Bren would become a client there. CVRC informed Jodie that early intervention services would change after Bren turned three years old. He was a month shy of turning three, when he received his diagnosis. At that time Jodie didn't know what any of this meant.

She trusted what she was told, and upon recommendation, she sought out *applied behavior analysis (ABA)*. Psychology Today, describes ABA as a type of therapy that focuses on improving specific behaviors, such as social skills, communication, reading, academics, adaptive learning skills, and more (2020). Jodie and her husband had toured some ABA providers, and then stumbled across a brand new program at *California State University, Fresno (CSUF)*. Dr. Amanda Nicolson, psychologist and *BCBA-D*, had just started the program. Jodie and her husband took a tour at the ABA center and knew right away, they had found the right place for their son. The only downside was that the new ABA program at CSUF, was not yet contracted with CVRC. This meant it wasn't an option just yet for the Howards.

Bren's parents had a hard decision to ponder. Should they wait until the program became a vendor; delaying the start of services and losing months of intervention time? Or, should they look for another program to start immediately, with no guarantee to match the same quality of service? Jodie says that they prayed about it and decided to wait. She believes it was the right decision. Jodie was happy to have Bren start services with Dr. Nicolson.

This is something Bren's parents have never regretted. Dr. Nicolson has been a pioneer in bringing stellar ABA services to the Central Valley. She's a great support in the autism community and to the Fresno Autism Network.

Around that same time, the Howards were living near the city of Fowler, CA. There were no *autistic like behavior (ALB)* preschool classrooms existing in the area. Bren was eligible to receive a total of 40 hours per-week, of early intervention services. Fortunately, their school district was able to fund for Bren to receive more hours at the ABA center to count toward the 40 hours, since there was no preschool placement option available within their district. Bren started intervention services receiving 20 hours funded through CVRC, and 20 hours through the school district. This continued through his first year of intervention.

The following year, when Bren was four years old, there was an ALB preschool program developed in the area. Bren attended the preschool. He also continued receiving ABA cervices at the autism center, for the other half of his day. Bren had a great start at early intervention. That's truly amazing considering that's not always the case for kids with autism. Unfortunately, the common reality is that parents often have to advocate hard, and fight tough battles to get services started for their children.

Bren's Autism

At four years old — (get this), Jodie and her husband found out that Bren could READ! The Howards had been teaching Bren sign language for a while. On a whim, Jodie wanted to test Bren, and see if he would make the appropriate signs for words he was given. She showed him hand written words on flash cards, with no pictures. It was a long-shot, but surprisingly Bren signed every single word on the cards, correctly!

Later, when Bren was around ten years old, they began trying to transition him to typing. Unfortunately, the whole world doesn't know sign language, which Bren was becoming fluent in. Go figure! Surprisingly again, the hardest part wasn't the typing! In fact, they NEVER had to teach Bren *how* to type, read, or spell. He simply picked it up on his own. The hardest parts were teaching him the give and take, along with other rules of communication, Jodie explained.

Bren is a sweet boy. He is accepting of everyone, and only has minimal behaviors that warrant concern. Although he is nonverbal, he does communicate. Today Bren uses sign language and typing to communicate. Impressively, he can now memorize entire movie scripts and type them out, word for word. I find that incredible! *Hold on Mr. Independence!*

Aside from communication, Bren still requires assistance in understanding other things, like rules for safety. Jodie still doesn't quite trust that Bren won't dart off in places, like parking lots, for example. She has to hold on to him. When he was little, she would have to hold Bren's hand to keep him safe. Now that he's older, Bren doesn't like that, he strives for independence. He always gets the choice in those situations to "link arms" or "hold hands". He much prefers to "link arms". Jodie loves knowing that her son has a desire for independence. That motivates her to provide him with as many opportunities for independence as possible. Like most mothers, she recognizes both her son's strengths and weaknesses. Jodie also has the opportunity, special to parents of children with disabilities; to see just how far her son has developed and progressed, since his diagnosis. Bren has definitely made huge strides! He certainly has come a long way from the earlier years, when Jodie was trying to figure out what was going on with him.

Candida You Say?

When Bren was six years old, Jodie and her husband, had come to find out that Bren had very bad *candida* in his gut. Candida is an overgrowth of yeast, which can lead to inflammation throughout the body. The Howards were seeing a doctor that used *holistic* approaches in treating Bren's candida. It was determined that Bren had very high levels in his body, of the hepatitis B vaccine, which is a vaccine given to babies after birth. The high levels of the vaccine present, must have been stewing around in his body for nearly five years, according to the doctor. His ammonia levels were very high as well. Bren's body couldn't expel all the toxins from the vaccines out.

Bren underwent a treatment that consisted of herbal medicines. This process took almost two years. The process also included restrictions of certain foods, like those containing wheat and milk. Another treatment option called, *Chelation* might have worked quicker. Chelation is a treatment involving administration of chelating agents to treat toxic metal poisoning (News-Medical.Net, 2019). Bren likely wouldn't have tolerated that process well, so the Howards opted for the less invasive route.

Jodie hoped that maybe Bren's language would start to develop after his gut was under control. It did not. The little bit of aggressive behavior he had, however, was mellowed out, Jodie explained.

Nonverbal Communication & Understanding

As Bren is nonverbal, expressions of thoughts are limited to a certain degree, even with use of alternative communication modes. Many times, educational assignments are set up in a way to demonstrate the child's receptive understanding, when they lack verbal language. A teacher or behavioral technician, may have the child point at pictures to answer questions, rather than trying to make the child say them or write them. That's just an example of how different communication styles can transcend to learning environments.

Getting just the right supports set up within a classroom for a nonverbal student like Bren, can be difficult. That doesn't mean it's impossible. It just requires a little thinking outside the box.

Complex conversations can also be difficult for Autistic or nonverbal children. For example, having a conversation with an Autistic child, about them having autism, can present its own challenges.

This could be a difficult thing to discuss with Bren, due to his autism, communication limitations, and level of understanding.

Does Bren know he has autism or that he's different than other people? The only way to truly answer that, would be to elicit a response from Bren, himself. Jodie says that she isn't really sure if he knows that he's different than other kids his age. She's not certain if he has a social understanding of that.

Should you tell your child/(ren) they have autism or not? The decision to tell a child with autism that they are *Autistic*, is split among the parents in our community. Again it can be difficult, due to communication and understanding barriers.

Nonetheless, Bren is surrounded by diverse populations. He's treated with dignity and respect by the people who are in his life. On top of that, he for sure has an amazing advocate in his corner, his mom!

Family Impact

Jodie's older sister continues to be a major support to her. Jodie looks up to her sister, and refers to her as, "one of the world's strongest women." Autism has made her extended family better people, according to Jodie. She shared that it has softened her own father, and has made him less quick to pass judgement on others. Jodie's father was of an older fashioned mindset; you teach your kids to behave, and if they don't, it reflects on the parents. He now realizes that for a child with autism, like two of his own grandchildren, that rule doesn't always apply! So for Jodie, even though her family doesn't live close by, they have become more tolerant and just better all around, with autism in their lives. Autism has been a blessing to her father, making him a better man, in her opinion. Jodie feels that autism has even made *her,* a better person.

As far as her husband's family is concerned, they are not very close. Of his family, her husband is closest with his mother. Jodie recognizes that her mother-in-law might be a little intimidated by autism. She shared that her mother-in-law, absolutely loves both Bren and his sister Sydney. Of the two, she tends to spend more time with Sydney. Bren doesn't reciprocate things like his younger sister. He doesn't express things in a typical manner to his grandmother. He doesn't clearly express for example, that he loves her, or what he wants for Christmas. It makes it a little difficult, leaving grandma not certain of what to do, or what to expect.

This is commonly experienced by many families living with autism, especially those with nonverbal or limited communicators. Perhaps it's misunderstanding? Ignorance? Or is it fear of difference? There's a possibility all those elements and others, play a role in the type of relationships that are formed within these families.

What She'd Do Different

If Jodie could have done anything differently, she says that she would have kept a better journal on her journey. There weren't phones with cameras available in the picture (no pun intended), when "the Bren" who didn't have autism existed. Though it was brief, Jodie wishes she could *really* remember that time, to track the transition more from no autism, to all the undeniable symptoms present. She doesn't remember where the dates line-up. When parents ask about the *measles mumps and rubella (MMR) vaccine,*[1] or any other environmental triggers, she can't say for sure if those variables played a role in the development of Bren's autism. She doesn't know for certain.

As far as when they got the diagnosis and started being proactive, there's not anything she really feels they should've done differently. Jodie is sure that there were times when she could have maybe taken a break from therapies. Or the opposite, when not pushing through therapy on occasion. Those are her only subtle regrets.

Autism has brought about some of the most positive things in Jodie's life. It has specifically brought

[1]MMR Vaccine - Some parents and professionals suspect that autism is caused by this vaccine.

her a whole world of wonderful people including, therapists, friends, and other people with autism. These people have become fixtures in Jodies world, and otherwise, each one might have just remained a passerby. Jodie's outlook on life in general, has been positively impacted by autism. "I think more people need to be more like Bren," Jodie says. She added, "I think the world would be just such a better place, if more people where like my son."

If There Was A Cure

If there were a medicinal cure for autism, and Jodie had the choice to give it to Bren, she wouldn't do it. She'd be tempted, as she had previously discussed with her sister; due to the experiences their children might miss in life. Still, she would not give Bren the cure. Jodie doesn't feel that Bren needs "fixing". She believes that he is, who he's *meant* to be.

Faith is such a big part of Jodie's life. This is the path that, "Heavenly Father wanted for my son," Jodie said. She doesn't look back at the transition from Bren without autism, to having it, as a negative thing. She says that Bren has affected and changed many lives. "I really do think the world is a better place, because my son is here," Jodie stated wholehearted. Bren is an incredible spirit in his mothers eyes and many others share in this view as well.

The Enrichment of Autism

The biggest way autism has enriched Jodie's life she feels, has been in changing her perspective. She didn't realize how judgmental she was, until she felt all the judging eyes on

herself, in the scope of raising her son with special needs. She realizes now, that she might have thought something similar to what the people who pass judgement do, before autism became part of her world. Now when Jodie sees people that are different shapes, sizes, colors, or behave differently, she doesn't even think about it twice! In those situations, where people are acting a little different from the "norm", it occurs to

Jodie that *maybe* — they have autism or another condition that affects their behavior.

Then there's the big one. *Acceptance.* Not just accepting people's differences, but actually celebrating them! Jodie says that she used to think she knew what acceptance was, but now she knows that she really didn't. She realized this as a result of Bren's autism.

Jodie's Perspective, & Message to Other Parents

Jodie sees autism as a very individualized thing, that is uniquely experienced by each person and family member living with the condition. According to Jodie, "We're in a similar realm, but on very different paths." Autism for Jodie has been difficult. At the same time, parts of it are easy. There's less drama, but in other ways there's more drama. A rollercoaster; never knowing if the day will be filled with ups and downs, or if it will go fast or slow. It has definitely been experienced as quite a ride for Jodie.

Jodie's advice for other parents, simply sums up the keys necessary for life after a diagnosis. First, she suggests to drop the fear and to not be afraid! Jodie recommends that you should start working hard to find services that your child needs, even if some fear remains. Finally, Jodie urges parents to keep pushing forward, and to stay proactive for their families. She believes that you have to give yourself some time to morn, however, getting stuck there is not in your best interest. You do need to make time for self-care as well. You have to forge forward. I couldn't agree with her more! Finally, Jodie cautions parents,"buckle up, because you're on a rollercoaster," she says.

Today Jodie is a fierce advocate for her son and other children with autism. Her experience and determination has led her to law school, and to graduate at the top of her class. Jodie is now a special-eduction attorney, in the Central Valley.

My Take

Looking at Jodie's story, I can't help but notice many similarities between her son and mine. They're both nonverbal, which is a subgroup itself, within the autism community. Jodie reminds us of some very noteworthy lessons. When I think about her expectation, and waiting to hear Bren's voice, wondering at one time what it would sound like, I'm brought to tears. Those tears quickly subside when she shares how she embraces her child, as he is. She gives some excellent examples of teaching Bren, the way that *he* learns. Jodie also touches on the importance of faith in her life, and how that has helped her shape her perspective of her son's autism. Some real truths are included in her story as well, regarding impacts of autism, as it relates to family dynamics.

Jodie described the disconnect between Bren and some family members. This stood out to me, because of how common it is to hear about the strain that autism can put on relationships, within immediate and extended families. Possible reasons why this occurs were mentioned, such as fear, lack of understanding, or ignorance. This issue makes me realize again, how critical it is to promote awareness and acceptance, not only in the general community, but within our own families.

I'm reminded through this story, to never giving up hope. Also, I'm reminded of how these kids can unexpectedly surprise us with their abilities, when given the right platform. It was so fascinating to me when Jodie explained about Bren's ability to type entire movie scripts from memory. Oh, and his ability to use sign language, that is incredibly impressive!

I sometimes share with Jodie about my son's newly discovered signs, when they pop up, because I know she can appreciate them. Jodie has definitely helped me in shifting my own perspective when it comes to communication expectations for my son. This story demonstrates strength, growth, unconditional love, and acceptance. Acceptance is key to being proactive, especially in a life with autism, in my opinion. The perception Jodie shared, that she believes Bren is exactly "who he's meant to be", stood out to me as the perfect example of acceptance. She's also found that "unique beauty" her sister said she would, in a world with autism in it.

CHAPTER 2

Lifeline

About five years ago, I met a woman named Claire at an autism parent support group. Claire was a mom of five children, which was one more child than I had at that time. I have since surpassed her, ha! We got to talking and found that we had quite a bit in common. Since then, we've stayed in touch through social media.

Claire and I sometimes bounce ideas off each other, regarding things like mountainous piles of laundry, and making the most out of small spaces for large families. I consider Claire a friend. She's one of the only other mothers I know, which I can relate to in regards to family size and special needs included. Like myself, Claire's got a jam-packed schedule full of school drop-offs and pick-ups, doctor appointments, and therapies. After that comes penciling in a date night, if there's room, and a sitter available (qualified for chaos). I appreciated that she spent nearly three hours with me for this interview.

I only waited about five minutes before Claire arrived at the Starbucks where we arranged to meet. She was wearing a long green dress with pink flowers on it. Her hair was tied back, she seemed slightly frazzled and a little nervous. Claire explained that prior to our meeting, she had spent a good deal of time on the phone trying to fix a problem with her son's insurance. We all know how stressful that can be! Then, on her way to our meeting, after a few minutes of driving, she realized she was headed in the wrong direction. I completely understood and assured Claire that it was okay. We sat at a little table in the corner of the coffee shop. Claire and I talked about our children, and the latest developments in our families. We commented on how strange it was being there without any of the handful of children we both have. After some catching up, I went through my list of questions with Claire.

Claire's Backstory

As mentioned, Claire is a mother of five children. She has two sons and three daughters. Both of her boys, Adam and Sean, have autism spectrum disorder (ASD). At the time of our interview Adam was ten years old and Sean was eight years old. I too have boys the same age, one of which is Autistic.

Some folks are surprised to learn that parents choose to have more children after a child is diagnosed with autism. Others think it's wonderful that siblings could be potential helpers, for the Autistic child throughout their lives. Claire and I can attest to that, both of us having more children younger than their siblings with special needs. We can see how the younger ones seem to just fall into uninstructed roles of "helpers".

A Complicated Pregnancy

During Claire's pregnancy with her first born, Adam, unforeseen circumstances developed. Her pregnancy wasn't anything like a first-time mother would expect. It definitely wasn't mapped out for Claire in the text books. To put it mildly, her pregnancy was rather complicated.

The first complication during Claire's pregnancy, was when she learned that she had *gestational diabetes*. If you haven't heard of it, gestational diabetes is a form of diabetes which is often temporary and can sometimes develop during pregnancy. Then at twenty-two weeks pregnant, Claire was in a car accident! She was fortunate to be alive and sustained only minor injuries. After the incident Claire started having pre-term contractions. This must have been awful!

Claire was given a medication called *Nifedipine* to stop the contractions. This was a very scary situation. Having a baby is life changing in and of itself, then add this on top of everything! Poor Claire was already having to cope with a whirlwind of emotions early into her pregnancy. At thirty-three weeks pregnant, Claire and her family received some terrible news. Through the use of a *fetal magnetic resonance imaging (MRI)* scan, doctors found a tumor in baby Adam's abdomen. This was before he was even born!

Life didn't get any easier when Adam was born. The tumor had metastasized to his liver. Adam's life was on the brink. He started *chemo-therapy* at only five days old. He was just an infant! Soon after, he had major surgery for the tumor. Adam stayed at the hospital for treatment during his first year of life. They lived in the hospital for most of that time, making it tuff for the entire family. To make matters worse, the chemo-therapy damaged Adam's hearing. His life was saved, but his hearing was not. Adam was left profoundly hearing impaired.

Due to his hearing loss he'd miss high pitched consonant sounds. Claire and her family were staying afloat by hanging on to their faith. Their hope for Adam's health was their primary focus. Very specific measures were taken to keep him safe and healthy in his delicate state.

Why is Adam Growling?

The complex struggles during her pregnancy with Adam, into his infancy, left some painful memories for Claire. Throughout her pregnancy she couldn't shake the thought that something else might be wrong, aside from the tumor. Claire said that she didn't know if it was a "God thing, or a motherly instinct, or both." After Adam was born, little by little, Claire's suspicions were confirmed.

At four months old, Adam started making strange growl-like vocalizations. This was different than cooing made by other four-month-old babies. When he was a little bit older, he displayed hypertonic muscle tone. Hypertonic muscle tone, or *hypertonia*, means that there is an excess of muscle in the arms and legs, making them stiff and difficult to move. Adam's body was very stiff, Claire explained. He would also walk on the tips of his toes (*toe walking*). He had severe oral aversions and was speech delayed, among other peculiarities. These were

48

the most unusual things Claire had ever seen in a young child. Claire had a degree in the field of child development, and had experience working with children. Drawing from that experience, she was certain that something about Adam's development wasn't quite right. She was determined to get to the bottom of her son's odd behavior. Masked by his major medical health issues at that time, it was quite the challenge to convince anyone that Adam's behavior wasn't normal. Still, Claire knew he needed attention.

Claire's family didn't believe Adam had anything else impeding on his development, other than his medical issues. Even after witnessing some of his odd behaviors, they still didn't share Claire's concern. She chalked up her family's dismissiveness to them being "old fashioned" and not liking to "read into things." At the same time, some of her family members and her doctors, attributed Claire's concern for Adam to her possibly being depressed. She agreed to some extent. Claire felt that the stress of being a new mother, combined with her concern for Adam's health, could very well have influenced her perception at that time. However, she was still convinced there was more going on with her son.

Claire wondered why traditional therapies for deaf and hard of hearing children, weren't working for Adam. He wasn't talking and he wasn't improving. When Adam was almost three years old, Claire decided to have him evaluated through the *Central Valley Regional Center (CVRC)*. She did this for peace of mind, and to feel validated.

The results were in! Claire wasn't the least bit surprised. She learned that Adam did in fact have something else going on. It wasn't simply that he was struggling to talk due to his hearing impairment. It was much more complex than that. Adam was diagnosed with *autism spectrum disorder (ASD)*.

The Truth Will Set You Free

Claire finally felt validated! She could finally start to get the right kind of help for her son.

She could now start to separate the two; his autism symptoms and his health issues.

After the diagnosis Claire decided to take Adam's hearing aides out. She thought, "his autism is so bad — these hearing aides are just amping him up, forget it!" Claire realized that the benefits of removing the hearing aides outweighed the benefits of leaving them in for Adam at that time. His sensory issues impeded on the effectiveness of the hearing aides. Once these measure were taken, Adam started progressing, and eventually started talking. At a little over six years old, Claire decided to reintroduce the hearing aides into Adam's routine. This time it was a success!

Despite the small victories, life was still difficult for Claire and her family. The early years were incredibly hard, she shared. Claire said, "those were the hardest years of not knowing what to expect." Having to submit to the unknown is difficult for many people all together. Add autism to your life, and it can bring more uncertainty of what the future holds.

Claire, like so many parents, had to learn all about what autism meant for her son. Autism wasn't something she was the least bit prepared for. Although she knew about his medical complications prior to Adam's birth, the thought of disability NEVER entered her mind. Claire said, "I did all the testing," and she never thought she'd have a child with a disability. Claire believes that nothing is set in stone. "You can't guarantee anything in this life," she said. It's true! You can't guarantee whether or not your child will have autism.

Services

Adam began services to help with his autism symptoms immediately following his diagnosis. He started receiving *applied behavior analysis (ABA)*, and *occupational therapy (OT)*. These are therapies routinely used with Autistic clients. They aim to reduce the problem behaviors associated with autism spectrum disorder, and replace them with non-harmful ones, that are socially appropriate. It took time, but Adam started making progress in many areas. However, treatment for

Adam's oral aversions were not going so well. After exhausting traditional therapies to treat his severe oral aversions, it was decided that Adam would use a *gastrostomy tube* (g-*tube*). He is now g-tube dependent. His g-tube has been a huge blessing in Claire's view. G-tube feeding for Adam is part of his family's daily routine. This is something that his entire family has gotten used to.

One Memorable Event

Over the years many situations related to Adam's autism, have left impressionable memories for his family. One of those particular eventful experiences, took place in the family's own backyard. Claire decided to let her children play out back. She watched from a window inside the house. She was sitting on their couch, holding the youngest of her kids and could see her other children playing outside. Everything was safe and enclosed. Claire convinced herself it was okay to relax a little bit. As she was getting more comfortable, Adam's siblings ran inside to tell her that Adam had just taken off all of his clothes! This happened within a split second. This is exactly the sort of thing Claire was afraid might happen!

To make matters worse, the neighbor's young daughter happened to witness Adam's disrobing. Claire was mortified! The neighbor was in law enforcement to top it all off. Claire felt she needed to go over and explain about her son having autism. She really didn't want her neighbors to draw any crazy conclusions about her family, based on their daughter's sighting. Her neighbors were sweet and completely understanding when Claire went over and attempted to excuse her son's behavior. That was a huge relief for her! Adam is better about keeping his close on, now that he's a little older.

Disrobing, or as I like to call it, running around in their birthday suit, appears to be a common theme among children with autism. Claire and I are no strangers to the struggle of keeping clothes on our boys with autism. I told Claire about my son's "Houdini-like" removal of clothes. For years, (and even sometimes now) we struggled with this. We tried using clothes with things like; laces, zippers, belts, overalls, and more, with no success! It wasn't until we found shoes that my son couldn't get out of, that we had any success with keeping clothes on him. Claire specifically remembered trying clothes with buttons to keep Adam dressed, but he would always find a way out of the clothes pretty quickly. "They're like ninjas," she laughed.

Keeping clothes on Adam was one behavioral challenge among others. The experience with ABA was another challenge. Claire just wasn't very comfortable having people other than family, inside her home. She's always been a rather private person.

Then there was toilet training! This was extremely difficult for everyone involved. There were days during toilet training when Claire felt like she was, "never going to be normal again," she said. I completely empathized with her!

We've had extreme difficulties in toilet training my own son with autism. We have experienced everything from fecal accidents on the floor, to fecal smearing, and more. By God's grace he's nearly completely toilet trained. Scrubbing our carpets is no longer a full-time job. Oh yes — I remember those days CRYSTAL clear!

Nonetheless for Claire, compared to his autism related challenges, it's always been more difficult to manage Adam's compromised health. "The health stuff gets to me, believe it or not, more than the disability," Claire said. Currently Adam is doing quite well in all areas. Claire says that Adam is such a happy kid normally, which makes it difficult for her to see him not well and not happy.

I could relate yet again, because of my son's epilepsy on top of his autism. Medical health conditions and neurological disabilities like autism, are very different things. On days when my son has seizures, I might post things on social media to the affect that, I'd choose the autism over epilepsy any day. I have also expressed at those times, that I just want my happy, healthy, Autistic son back, quirks and all. The medical health issues are sometimes more difficult than the challenges of having autism.

Claire sees her son as a huge blessing, and just wants him well. I completely understand her position. Her wishes for her son are similar to the wishes of mothers of healthy, and health compromised children around the globe.

History Repeats Itself

Claire became well versed in special needs because of Adam. One thing she learned, is that some things might run in families. When she suspected symptoms of autism in her younger son Sean, she got him in for an assessment at CVRC right away. Sean also was officially diagnosed with autism spectrum disorder, when he was just shy of three years old.

With Sean, Claire and her husband wanted to try things a little differently than they did with Adam. They decided against special-education services. They started Sean a year later than his peers in kindergarten. Claire and her husband wanted to give Sean a little more time to develop, and be as learning-ready as possible. They delayed his start in preschool. Claire said,"I did the wrong thing, probably…his health is good, but socially, we struggle." Despite wondering if she did the right thing for Sean regarding his education, she is certain that he would have struggled a great deal more, should he had started school at grade level.

"You can tell that Sean has autism," Claire said. Although Sean is verbal, he can't answer questions without *prompting*, and he repeats what other people say. It was easier to get services started for Sean, since his older brother Adam was already receiving services. Somewhat of a roadmap was already paved. Even still, Claire felt similar to the way she felt regarding Adam's diagnosis. She felt unsupported by some family members and friends.

When Claire's concerns about Sean initially came up, others thought it was pure exhaustion, causing Claire to overthink things. Sure, life can be overwhelming with the demands of young children close together in age, but Claire had already been down this path with Adam. There was no denying that her family didn't recognize Sean's differences like she did. Could it be that it was more difficult for others to see the symptoms of autism in Sean, because he was verbal? Perhaps it was due to the fact that he didn't have the same complications his brother did. This trend made it easy for Claire to feel very alone and unsupported.

Isolation of Autism

Over the course of Claire's life with autism, she found herself isolated and lonely for several years. She had to keep her son Adam away from the outside world for some time; due to the delicate nature of his health at the start of her parental journey. Claire admits that she didn't have a strong set of coping skills during those early years, after Adam's cancer treatment. She still hadn't learned effective coping strategies when he was diagnosed with autism. She also thought she was perfectly fine and had a handle on everything. In thinking that way, "I did a disservice to my entire family," she said. "I got isolated when Adam was sick with cancer because we couldn't have visitors, we couldn't have germs,.. I became almost like a recluse…I was like, I need to stop, I can't be a recluse with kids, that's not healthy for kids," Claire said. Adam's medical situation made it easier for Claire to get in the habit of shutting herself and her family off from the world.

Isolation is a common struggle for those with autism, and their families. For many people with autism, it's easier to retract from the outside world to avoid becoming overwhelmed, experiencing sensory-overload, or anxiety. Many parents that are afraid to participate in "normal" social events, due to their feelings regarding their child's Autistic behaviors, can become depressed, isolated and anxious as well. The truth is that without being exposed, and learning to cope, many meaningful life experiences can be missed.

Claire had became isolated and exhausted, not only physically, but emotionally too. Her husband was supportive and worked incredibly hard to care for their family. What more could she ask for? She still felt alone, stirring in the hardship of being a stay at home mom of multiple children, including two with special needs. The stress was weighing on her immensely!

Most people have one person, someone, or something they turn to in the midst of trouble. Our voice of reason. Sometimes its our own conscience, and sometimes it's literally someone else's voice or spoken advise. There was a pivotal moment that changed the trajectory of Claire's life. It took a single phone conversation with the person who had known Claire her entire life. Her mother.

Asking for Help

Claire's saving grace was in her own mother's words, during that phone call. She realized something very important, something she hadn't considered before. As she recalls in this phone conversation, her mother said to her, "Claire, he can't read your mind!" It was such an eye opening statement! She realized that if she needed help, she needed to ask for it. She also realized that she had been keeping everything inside. Here she had a loving and supportive husband, who was always there for her. Yet, he didn't know what she needed because she never told him! Claire remembered thinking, "all he knows is his wife looks kind of cranky, and is kind of mumbling to herself, and stirring the spaghetti."

She decided to test it out. As soon as Claire approached her husband for help, she was pleasantly surprised with his responsiveness. She was blown away with knowing how the simple communication she had been withholding, made such a HUGE difference, in the level of support she would receive from him.

Finding Herself in Autism

Claire has since developed healthier coping strategies for dealing with her stress, anxiety, and isolation tendencies. Some of her new coping strategies include, change of perception and learning how to communicate. For a long time she was just happy Adam was alive. Now she is encouraging family involvement, appreciating, and participating in life. Also, Claire use to assume her husband knew what kind of help she needed. Now she is more vocal and specific about what support she needs from him.

Today Claire feels much happier in her family role. She recognizes how far she and her family have come in their lives with special needs. She is now more involved in her faith and with her community. Claire and her husband continue working together to maintain a happy, healthy home for their family.

My Take

Claire's story was eye opening for me. This has definitely been one complex journey for this mom and her family. Having two boys with autism myself, and one with a medical condition as well, I can relate somewhat. Claire found strength within herself to keep pushing forward, doing the best she could, even when others didn't believe she knew what was right. This brings to light the importance of following your instincts. We are the experts on our own children.

As parents, we are not perfect nor do we claim to be. I'm grateful for Claire's honesty in explaining her and her husband's decisions, regarding their approach to their younger son Sean's education. A few things came to mind for me surrounding this part of the story. First, time is precious and of the essence when we look at intervention. Claire took a huge leap of faith in not pushing for early intervention services for Sean the same way she did for Adam. I admire her confidence in making that decision. There were definite pros and cons to it that she explained. Also having a child on the spectrum who is less severe than his older brother myself, I can relate to her rationale. Overall I am a huge supporter of early intervention.

I think another major thing to remember, is how easy it can be to lose yourself in motherhood. Claire was no exception there. She lost herself in her role as a special-needs mother. Her saving grace was in that phone call with her own mother. She was reminded to use her voice to communicate with her husband, because he couldn't read her mind. I find this to be an incredibly valuable lesson. It's essential to know when to ask for help, to be brave enough to do so, and to be specific in the kind of help you're asking for. Claire's story reminds me of the importance of using our voices when we are able, as we advocate for those who are not. In this case, Claire was needing to use her voice as her lifeline, from the isolation hole she fell into. Communication was the key to her healing. Lastly, Claire is a fine example of making light of hard situations, and acclimating to a life with special needs.

CHAPTER 3

Overcomer

Before marriage, parenthood and special needs came into my life, I worked at a child development center in our local school district. I made plenty of friends and acquaintances. I crossed paths with Carolyn, a parent of kids attending the school I worked at. Years later when autism came into my life, we crossed paths again.

Carolyn met me at a coffee shop for our interview. She arrived before I did and waited at a table for me. It was a little noisy, but when the recorder started rolling all the other sounds started to fade away. We then dived into her story.

I had seen some of Carolyn's struggles with autism first handedly at events, when her son was much younger. So, getting the opportunity to hear about the last few years, that's something I couldn't pass up! I was extremely interested to hear the story of her child, who is also nonverbal like my own son.

About Carolyn

Carolyn is happily married. She has her seventeen-year-old step-son Jacob, her daughter Allison, also seventeen, and her thirteen-year-old son Benny. Life wasn't always pretty. In fact, Carolyn never thought that her life could resemble what it does now. Her story is one of strength and perseverance. She faced the challenges of betrayal, loss, and heartbreak, as you will discover as you continue reading.

The Story Begins

What seems like another lifetime ago, Carolyn was pregnant from her high school sweetheart. Sadly, he passed away before their daughter Allison was born. When Allison was two years old, Carolyn met and started dating Andy. The couple got married and had their son Benny. Eventually the couple would split up.

Benny's Development

Benny was developing typically until he was one and a half years old. He would do things like, pretend to talk on a toy phone and play with toy cars, "and then it all kind of stopped," Carolyn said. Other little things started to stand out to Carolyn regarding her son's development. Benny had been a good eater up until that point. He had a fairly well balanced diet, eating plenty of fruits and vegetables. That stopped too! He only wanted to drink milk. Changes that didn't quite add up, were stacking up.

Carolyn doesn't remember exactly when, but one of her biggest concerns arose when Benny stopped responding to his name being called. She was worried about how he would sit for long periods of time, holding his hand on the side of his head, and stare off into space. She started to believe that there must be something wrong with him. First, she thought that maybe he had a bad ear infection. Then, she wondered if maybe he was having trouble hearing. Carolyn ended up taking Benny to the doctor to find out what exactly was going on. The pediatrician kept insisting nothing was wrong with Benny, but Carolyn didn't agree. She remained persistent. Eventually, he made a referral for Benny to a children's hospital, for auditory testing.

According to the test results, Benny's ears were functioning fine. He had a little fluid behind one ear, but nothing significant enough to affect his hearing. The children's hospital, then made a referral for Benny to the *Central Valley Regional Center (CVRC)*. At CVRC, Benny would be assessed for *autism spectrum disorder (ASD)* and other developmental conditions.

Knowing that Benny was being assessed for autism, Carolyn tried to wrap her mind around the idea of her child possibly being Autistic. She explained that she had one idea in her mind about autism. That idea was a stereotype and a misguided one. It was a grim and terrifying misunderstanding she had. Initially, Carolyn believed autism was ALL severe, crazy, frightening, and extremely negative. She was convinced there was NO WAY her son had that dreadful condition!

It wasn't until she researched autism herself, and was able to better understand it, that Carolyn accepted the possibility that Benny might be Autistic. She actually felt relieved to think that there was a name for what was going on with him. It could explain his difficulties and differences. She also learned that there were therapies and interventions, designed specifically to help people with ASD.

Benny's grandmother had watched a Spanish documentary about a boy with autism. The boy in the documentary had extreme behaviors and had been locked in a room. This resulted in a skewed understanding of autism for Benny's grandma, similar to what Carolyn initially thought about autism. When Carolyn tried to explain the condition to Benny's grandmother and to other family members, it wasn't always well received. They seemed convinced that autism was all one way, like the boy in the documentary.

Carolyn knew better now. It's common to hear about extended family members not "getting it", when it comes to truly understanding autism within their family.

It was through CVRC, when Benny was three years old, that he received an official diagnosis of autism spectrum disorder (ASD). It wasn't too hard a pill to swallow for Carolyn, because in the back of her mind, she was already expecting it. It was however, difficult to discuss with Benny's grandmother, due to her perception of autism, based on that documentary she watched. Another thing that was extremely difficult for Carolyn, was the label given to Benny by his school a few years later.

In school, Benny was labeled with *intellection disability*. Intellectual Disability, or ID, means that a person has a less than average *IQ score*, and requires a great deal of functional living assistance. More than the autism, Carolyn was terrified about what this label meant for her child. Would he ever get married? Would he have children? Would he be able to live independently as an adult? Would he be taken advantage of? These were some of the many questions that Carolyn had.

The Hard Work of a Special-Needs "Married Single Mother"

During her marriage to Andy, and after Benny's initial diagnosis, Carolyn was overwhelmed. She was juggling work, child care, and searching for answers to best help her son. Often, she felt very alone in her marriage, as there was so much divide surrounding the topic of autism between her, Andy, and his family. Carolyn and Andy both worked in a school setting; Carolyn as a teacher, and Andy as a custodian. Being that Carolyn brought in a higher income, it was decided that Andy would stay home to watch their children, and she would work. This was the only way Carolyn thought they could make ends meet, and have someone care for Benny in the way he needed. Carolyn was a little uneasy about this decision, but she felt happy that her daughter would be there. She would be able to help her step-father with little things for Benny.

There was a lot of friction and fighting with Benny's father's family, especially. It got increasing worse, not better. Their way of handling Benny's diagnosis, was different than Carolyn's. She was determined to help her son, so that's where her focus remained, despite the lack of familial support.

After receiving his diagnosis, Carolyn was referred by the local school district to an early intervention placement for Benny. This program was intended for children with language and developmental delays. Benny also received speech therapy.

Carolyn wanted to help her son "get better". She got the impression from the speech therapist, that Benny would be able to talk one day. Carolyn said, "my expectation was that he was gonna one day wake up, and just be able to talk." She held on to that hope, and it was her driving motivation for a long time. Carolyn dove into this new endeavor, trying to find the right doctors, therapists, and anything under the sun that could help improve her son's condition.

She followed fad theories for a while. These theories promised to make Autistic children "better". Why wouldn't she try it for her son? At one time, she changed Benny's diet to exclude dairy. This diet showed some improvement for a period of time. A notable decrease in sensory issues, was the biggest improvement for Benny with eliminating dairy. It did not, however, rid him of his autism.

The Beginning of Public Education

As Benny entered public education in an *autistic like behavior (ALB)* preschool classroom, Carolyn was simultaneously working with him on behaviors such as; *eloping,*[2] jumping out of windows, and more. After that year, Benny transferred to another school for first grade, into another ALB classroom. At that time, his behaviors were a little more severe, including; screaming, kicking, hitting, bitting, and tripping. Benny needed more support. Although the programs were set up for children

---

[2] Eloping - refers to when an Autistic child quickly runs off unsupervised from any location.

with autism, it seemed as though the way autism affected Benny, didn't fit the bill. Being that the school did not adequately provide effective services for Benny, Carolyn took it upon herself to find learning tools for children with ASD, suitable for her own son. The fact that she was a teacher, was immensely helpful in her search for resources.

She requested an evaluation from the *assistive technology (AT)* person, so that her son could start building communication skills in school, with use of an iPad and proper applications. After the assessment Carolyn was told that Benny didn't qualify. They told her he wasn't ready.

Carolyn disagreed with the school district. She knew that Benny was fluent with the *Picture Exchange Communication System (PECS)*, and was ready to transition to an iPad.

According to National Autism Resources, PECS allows limited communicators to communicate by using pictures. They are taught to approach another person, giving them the picture of a preferred object, in exchange for the object (2020).

Carolyn took it upon herself, purchased an application called *Proloquo 2 Go*, and started teaching her son on her own. She then reached out directly to the AT person and got a reevaluation done for Benny. Benny was then approved for an iPad in school. He was one of the first students in the ALB classroom to get an iPad. CVRC reimbursed Carolyn for the application she had independently purchased for Benny as well. Sometimes, we have to do just as Carolyn did, believe when no one else is willing to. Then, fight like crazy!

Despite that victory, Benny was still having a really hard time in school. Carolyn remembers after the struggle of drop-off, sitting in her car and just crying her eyes out. That is so hard! How many of us haven't been there?

She knew her son needed to be in school, but her heart ached for her baby boy. It was torture making him stay, when she knew he absolutely didn't want to. As special-needs parents, we have to grow tough skin, and there's no way around that. When you come across other parents doing the same thing knowing how difficult it is, you actually kind of feel empowered. When you get educators who look at you and recognize that you know what you're doing, nodding at how bad a$$ you are in that tough moment, there's no better feeling in the world! That however, is few and far between.

You know that one teacher all parents of special-needs children dream about? It's the one who is brave enough to advocate for your child, and see past their challenging behaviors. Well, the silver lining was that Benny actually had one of those. This teacher would sit out in the parking lot with Benny, acknowledging his feelings and talking to him. She was compassionate and kind, understanding, and above all, patient. This teacher made an impression on Carolyn.

Then, something new started happening. At the time, Benny didn't have "feelings" in his vocabulary. Independently, he started to press the icon on his iPad that said, "scared". Benny was scared! Ugh! This was wildly bittersweet. Aside from learning that Benny was feeling scared, both he and his mom learned, he could communicate more than just basic wants with his iPad. This was an incredible development for Benny. Carolyn was very happy to see her son progressing and showing her more of what he was capable of.

Despite the increasing communicative progress, Benny's behaviors continued to be extreme. Carolyn tried *applied behavior analysis (ABA)* for Benny. After being in ABA for some time, Carolyn didn't see any progress. ABA wasn't bringing anything new to the table. It caused a lot of frustration for Benny and her. It was a very difficult time for everyone. Carolyn continued to seek out resources to help her manage her son's behaviors and increase his communication.

After third grade, Carolyn started a new teaching job and Benny moved to another school. This was a big transition for everyone. Carolyn continued working, and her husband continued watching the kids. She was grateful despite the challenges. She was happy as long as her kids were happy. Her daughter Allison was a Godsend. She never gave her mom any problems, and was a good sister to her little brother.

The Good Sister

Allison and Benny have always been close. Allison has always looked out for her little brother. She has been instinctively nurturing from a young age.

There was a time when Allison was around five years old, and Benny happened to wander outside of their house into the front yard. Carolyn was putting something away and turned her attention away from the kids for just a split second. When she looked up from what she was doing, she then caught a glimpse of the kids outside, and raced out to get them. Allison was guiding her little brother inside already. It was a scary ordeal. Allison explained to her mom that she saw Benny go outside, she didn't know where he was going carrying his favorite pillow, but she knew she needed to get him. This young child instinctively felt responsible for her little brother's safety. She didn't wait to tell her mom. She reacted and immediately assumed a parent-type role. This was just one of the first examples of how much responsibility, Allison would feel she needed to carry for her little brother with special needs. Allison would offer help whenever needed. Carolyn was amazed by the regard her daughter possessed at such a young age.

Even though there was still tension in her marriage regarding Benny's condition, Carolyn kept working hard. Knowing her kids were in the care of her husband, Benny's father, was reassuring to Carolyn. Carolyn thought that this plan was okay. Why shouldn't she? Unfortunately things aren't always as they seem. Life's not a dream, and sometimes it can feel like a really bad one, a nightmare.

A Parent's Worst Nightmare

It had been no more than two weeks into the new school year, when Carolyn was contacted by her daughter's school. A police officer and a *Child Protective Services (CPS)* worker, were waiting to meet with her.

Her heart raced as she drove over to Allison's school. A million terrible thoughts raced through her mind. She honestly feared they'd tell her that one of her babies were dead.

Allison and Benny were alive, thank God! Carolyn was relieved but not for long. Allison had confided in a friend at school about a deep dark secret she had been living. This friend convinced Allison to come forward with the shocking news. Carolyn's world was about to be shaken. With all the challenges she faced in her life, she never imagined something like this would happen. As it turns out, Allison had been molested and raped by her step-father, Benny's father Andy! The abuse took place several times over the years.

Carolyn was in disbelief, and she was devastated! A mixture of pain, guilt, anger, and more, came over this mother. A mother who only wanted to help her children the best way she knew how to. The one person she had no reason to doubt, and trusted with all her heart, violated her very essence! He had every opportunity, as he was the parent that was supposed to be taking care of the kids. He took so much from Allison, and Benny was a witness to some of the abuse.

Carolyn will never know if Benny too was abused in any other way. Due to his condition, he can never be considered a witness in court. When she asked her daughter why she didn't come to her for help, Carolyn remembers her daughter tearfully saying, "who was going to take care of Benny? You have to work, and Benny can't go to a babysitter or daycare like other kids." Carolyn felt helpless and broken for her children.

Allison put her brother's safety before her own. She felt she had to make a choice. Brother's safety or hers. With autism in the mix, she chose to endure the abuse to keep her brother safe. I can't even imagine the torment she endured! Learning of the wrongful, shameful acts imposed on this innocent child, and her astronomical bravery, left me speechless.

Allison has worked through an abundance of horrific experiences, no child should ever have to.

Amazingly she continues to look out for her little brother. As the kids have grown, Carolyn has witnessed many times that Allison would like to be with her friends, but often chooses her brother instead, despite her mother's encouragement.

Now, Allison was a senior in high school, and little brother Benny, a Freshman. Allison came home excitedly after getting her class schedule. She wanted to inform her mom that she took an elective in which she would be in her brother's classroom on certain days. Carolyn says that Allison has always been willing to help her brother, without complaint. This stood out to Carolyn as different and special about her daughter; when other kids might complain, or would rather be doing something else.

Allison wants to become a psychologist. I think she'd make an absolutely incredible one at that! She is a perfect example of healthy healing after trauma.

Backing up just a little bit to the dramatic turn of events, Andy was arrested and sent to jail. Benny was having an extremely hard time at his new school. Despite the horrible things that his father had done, Benny's world was turned upside down. He would ask for his dad over and over some days. Carolyn let Benny have visits with his father's family for a time, but then it became too much for Benny. He would become confused about everything, and miss his father all over again. Things got even worse, and got to a point where Carolyn had to file a restraining order against Andy's family. After that, they cut all ties and tried to move on with their lives. All the while, Carolyn was receiving frequent phone calls from the elementary school where Benny attended. Can you imagine? It was an excruciating and terrible time for this family! The school didn't have all the details about what was happening with home life.

When it Rains it Pours

The phone calls home continued. With multiple teachers in the classroom, and a low ratio of students, Carolyn couldn't comprehend how with all the support, they couldn't help her son on their own. They weren't dealing with situations that weren't already addressed in his *Individualized Education Plan (IEP)*.[3] Carolyn thought she might lose her job, as she was frequently contacted at work, having to leave to go to the school on many occasions. Benny was having terrible meltdowns. Carolyn didn't get any straight answers from the school. This left her to believe that most of the behavior was influenced by the major changes at home.

Then one day, Benny's grandmother went down to the school to pick him up for Carolyn. What she found was rather disturbing. The teacher had locked Benny inside the classroom as he was having a serious meltdown. Carolyn's mother called her to come down to the school immediately! The principal explained to Carolyn that the teacher did this for the safety of the other children. Carolyn wanted to know what happened that evoked her sons meltdown. Eventually, she found out that the teachers were letting Benny sleep for long

[3] IEP- The education plan for students with special needs, receiving special-education.

periods of time during the school day. He was agitated and grumpy when he was woken up. Carolyn felt that they allowed him to sleep, because it was easier than them having to "deal with him". In Carolyn's opinion, the classroom staff had a huge part to play in triggering his major meltdown.

Benny ended up being suspended, and the school was never able to determine if his major meltdown when he was locked in the classroom, was a result of his condition or not. This was essential in justifying suspension. Carolyn felt that his meltdown was completely a result of his condition, in response to what the staff allowed, and didn't allow her son to do. She feels that his escalation would have been avoided with the proper supports in place. Those supports were actually stipulated in his IEP. So many things were wrong with this placement aside from that incident, according to Carolyn. They reported that Benny only knew one word for example, when Carolyn knew he could read and write many words. No one believed her

— his mother! She had to call a few emergency IEP meetings that school year.

Carolyn recalls sitting at her last IEP meeting at this school. She was completely beside herself, zoned out, stopped listening, and just sat there as everyone talked. They sat there talking about her son, and providing presumptions about her child. This is the same child, that she had worked tirelessly with and for. *Her* child, who had been through so much trauma. Carolyn was done.

After that school year, she moved Benny back to the school he was at before. She was happy to get him out of there. I think I would be too.

You Won't Know Unless You Try, and Try Again, and Again, and Again…

Moving Benny back to the prior school he had transitioned from, was the best decision Carolyn feels she made. Benny now had the structure he needed and he had a good teacher. Benny made massive strides in his reading level in one school year. This was a little ironic, being that the prior school claimed that Benny could only read one word. That was not true! The classroom now was a good fit for Benny, and it reflected in his progress and behavior. Carolyn's IEP meeting went much smoother this time around.

Since the incident surrounding Benny's father was somewhat behind them now, Carolyn was ready to start getting proactive again. Looking at that horrible experience with his father, Carolyn realized even more so, just how important Benny's communication was. She wanted to make sure that Benny's voice was always with him. She never wanted him to be in a vulnerable situation, without a means of communication again. Carolyn emphasizes the importance of Benny having his iPad for communicative purposes in every IEP. He hasn't been without his device since.

A Shift in Perspective

Carolyn worked diligently helping her family to recover from their trauma, and she was ready to take the bull by the horns, in a matter of speaking. She adopted a slightly new view. She realized after all the years, that she couldn't "cure" the autism out of Benny, no matter how hard she tried. Accepting that autism isn't something to be cured, was a huge shift for Carolyn. She now researched ways to help provide her son the right supports for success, and happiness in his life. Since then, she has strived to help people see Benny the way that she does; capable, smart, funny, independent and full of love, just different. Carolyn's unconditional love for her children, is what has helped her overcome the challenges she's faced, in her life with a special-needs child. Carolyn's expectation of Benny's future, is much brighter now. She does hope that he always has someone that supports him in his life, who sees beyond his autism.

At school when someone waves at Benny in the hall, even if he doesn't respond, it warms Carolyns heart. Knowing that people accept him just as he is, is worth everything. Carolyn used to wonder about all the "what if's" regarding her son's future. She also spent countless hours exploring her guilt, regarding what her daughter went through. She has come to a place of acceptance, and believes wholeheartedly, that everything happens for a reason. Carolyn encourages other mothers, (who she sees on social media caught up in negativity) to look at the good things right in front of them. She feels bad for mother's stuck on the negative side.

Carolyn is re-married to a wonderful husband. She is fully supported and loved by those around her. Her children are as well. Carolyn's mother has been one of her greatest supports, even though they don't always see eye to eye. Carolyn's husband has been a great support as well, in helping her create a productive path for Benny. When she's lazy, he keeps her accountable.

Carolyn was a single mother for three years, and she didn't think she'd make it. She says that it was the hardest three years of her life. She met her husband and he pulled her out of the hole she was in. "He saved us," she said. Carolyn feels extremely blessed that Benny and her husband bonded. He helped provide structure where it was lacking, and she attributes a lot of Benny's success to that. Carolyn's husband has been an incredible father figure for Allison as well.

Benny is Growing up

Carolyn is learning to give Benny space. The once, completely dependent boy, has turned into a teenager who wants to be independent. Carolyn shared how they went to a trampoline park and she was kind of "*helicopter parenting*". Then Benny looked at her with his eyes saying "give me some space, mom." Another time, her family was at McDonalds. Benny ordered his food by himself, then proceeded to go to use the bathroom. Carolyn wanted to go in and check on him, but her husband stopped her. He reminded her that it was okay and that Benny knew what to do. Bittersweet, the developments and all the struggles have started to pay off. Carolyn is working on letting go…a little bit. As much as Benny wants to be independent and seen as a teenager, Carolyn wants that too. She doesn't want her children to be defined by autism or as victims. She continues to encourage them to strive for the same.

"Don't Lose Site of the Big Picture."

"It's been a crazy rollercoaster," Carolyn says. Her story truly illustrates that. Her son's condition isn't something she fears anymore. There have been more tears, sweat, and prayers than she can count. Still, as Carolyn and her family manage their way through life with autism in the middle, she likes to remind others by saying, "don't lose site of the big picture."

My Take

Carolyn's story was absolutely a rollercoaster of events. I was shocked and saddened by some of the most unbelievably compelling circumstances Carolyn shared. This story shed light on the sibling dynamic and resiliency of children. Allison presented such amazing character in such a horrific situation! She's a natural born protector and advocate. She was going to protect her brother at all costs, literally. It's a bitter sweet reality for Allison, and for many siblings of children with autism. They sometimes carry a weight created by the demands of their brothers or sisters with special needs.

Carolyn has instilled in her children that they are not victims or defined by labels. This takes practice and internalization. It's not always easy to adopt those values when family or friends don't quite understand. When she talks about the difficult decision to cut ties with family due to the toxic relationship, I am reminded of that reality for many autism parents. To have people understand autism itself is one thing, but add trauma, and that would be too much for most. It's not fair a lot of the time, but this is our reality.

This story brings up an important fact. Not all therapies work for every child, even some of the most commonly used ones like ABA. The key is to be proactive and make decisions based on what is best for your child.

Also, I'm reminded that there may come a point where my child with autism may seek independence. They grow and develop just like everyone else, at their own pace. That's easy to forget when you're in the thick of it, trying to teach them basic skills. I thought it was bittersweet when Benny indicated to his mom that he wanted to do things by himself.

Carolyn is an example of being a true overcomer with everything that has transpired on her journey with autism. She's never stopped fighting for her son, and the fight is paying off tremendously. Many times her faith only hung by a thread, but she sees all of the good in her life as blessings. I find her story incredibly inspiring! The last thing I'd like to mention is how inspiring her view on autism is. I love how she urges autism mothers not to get stuck in a bitter cycle. She encourages them to embrace their children, and do the best that they can.

CHAPTER 4

Karlye's Happy Bubble

This next story is about a single mother, named Beth. Beth is a second-grade school teacher. Beth has only one child, a daughter who's name is Karlye. At the time of our interview Karlye was eleven years old. Karlye has *autism spectrum disorder (ASD)* and is *nonverbal*. She attends public school. Karlye has also been given the label of *intellectual disability (ID)*. A label one might think is too quickly attached to students with autism.

Beth's daughter and my son attended some of the same therapy centers over the years. I was very interested in hearing all about Beth's journey raising a little girl with autism, as I only have boys on the spectrum. According to the Centers for Disease Control and Prevention, boys are more than four times more likely than girls to have autism (2019).

I think it's important to recognize that girls also have this condition. Autism doesn't discriminate, it touches all walks of life. Girls with autism require as much attention and support, as boys with the condition.

Coffee Chat

I met Beth at a coffee shop. Apparently coffee shops create a nice ambiance for hearing these amazing stories. I'm actually not a coffee drinker. Tea is my cup of tea (pun intended), haha! Beth proceeded to share her incredible journey with autism as we sat at our table.

When Beth was pregnant with Karlye, she envisioned her growing pregnant belly harboring a beautiful little girl, which it did. Being a teacher, she imagined her daughter excelling academically and being at the top of her class. Beth envisioned her daughter being the teacher's pet. She had imagined Karlye being the kid that went over and beyond; staying after school to help out. Beth couldn't have known what the future held for Karlye.

The Immunizations

When Karlye was sixteen months old, Beth took her to the doctor for immunizations. There were six shots in total given that day. Beth explained that Karlye, up until that time, would repeat words. She'd say words she had heard on tv; Dora, mama, dada, etc. She also had a healthy appetite. She would eat everything!
Meat and potatoes were just among some of the foods Karly enjoyed. Karlye would eat with utensils, and drink out of cup using a straw. She was curious and full of life! After those immunization, Beth says that her daughter changed.

Karlye immediately developed a fever and was sick for about a week! She lost interest in everything. She would crawl up on the couch and sit and stare off with a blank gaze. She wasn't eating anything now, except applesauce.With every fiber of her being, Beth knew that something wasn't right. Even when Karlye's grandmothers from both sides of the family would come to visit, they wondered about what had happened to Karlye. Beth described it as Karlye being a million miles away. Beth didn't know what to do! She was really scared for her daughter. It was a lot of change at once. She hoped that after the fever subsided, and she started feeling better, Karlye would bounce back to her typical adventurous self. Beth said, "She never came out of it." Karlye was a different kid. "If I didn't see it with my own eyes, I wouldn't believe it," Beth said. Beth suspected autism.

I couldn't help but well up with tears a little bit listening to this. Even with indifference in one's tone of voice in sharing a story told many times, these stories always takes us mothers back. Kind of stops you in your tracks for a minute. My son was different from day one. To have something and lose it, must have been incredibly painful for Beth to witness.

In the area of autism, there is much debate regarding what causes the condition. Some people have genetic mutations, and if injury occurs within an individual with such a condition, they may present with symptoms of autism. Specific genetic testing can be done to rule out genetic mutations. Beth shared that because of the difference of opinions between herself and Karlye's father, genetic testing was not an option. Due to Karlye's experience, she will not receive any further immunizations. However, Beth does not consider herself a complete *antivaxer.* She considers herself a cautious and informed decision maker. Beth suggests to friends that are pregnant, "one vaccine at a time." Like many parents, Beth trusted her pediatrician. She also didn't know about delayed immunizations, as a choice.

The Diagnosis and Start of Services

Karlye's father didn't validate Beth's concerns about their daughter. Being a teacher, working with kids, and knowing about the prevalence rate of autism then, Beth Scheduled testing anyway. Karlye was two years old when Beth took her to the *Central Valley Regional Center (CVRC)*for an autism assessment. They also went to another diagnostic center up north, where Karlye was initially given a diagnosis of *pervasive developmental disorder-not otherwise specified (PDD-NOS)*. PDD-NOS was a diagnosis given to children who presented some symptoms of autism, but not all.

The diagnostic center told Beth that this was the only label they could give Karlye because of her age. She was too young to be diagnosed with autism spectrum disorder, according to that diagnostic center. It sounded more like a money thing to Beth. PDD-NOS didn't get funding for services back then. Beth was devastated by the assessment findings. She realized the dreams she had for her daughter wouldn't happen in the same way, and possibly not at all.

Beth admits that after Karlye received her diagnosis, she wondered if she had anything to do with it in any way. Did she unknowingly cause this "autism" to happen? Did that Pepsi or hotdog craving during pregnancy have anything to do with it? After realizing there was really something changed in her perfect daughter, regardless of the cause, Beth knew her life wasn't going to be the same. This change had a name. This different way of life was called, *autism*.

Beth had to jump through hoops, so to speak. Nonetheless, Karlye received her clinical diagnosis of autism through CVRC that October. The following January she started in an in-home intervention program through a local school district.Unfortunately, it was unsuccessful. The program was ineffective and brought about worse behaviors, instead of improving the few that Karlye was struggling with. Karlye was now unwilling to even sit in a chair! The company used tools that may have worked for other children, but those tools weren't working for Karlye. They weren't meaningful to her. Perhaps it was the inability to modify, or lack of understanding of variance in the autism spectrum, that resulted in the program not being the right fit for Karlye. In every program they tried afterward, Beth would have to explain about what didn't work for her daughter previously. It was frustrating, to say the least.

Karlye's Parents started getting involved in the autism support community at that time. They regularly attended meetings with an organization called, *Talk About Curing Autism (TACA)* in Visalia, CA. The initial meetings were difficult for Beth. She found herself overwhelmed with emotion, having to step out if the meetings to cry at times.

Karlye's father and Beth learned some helpful tips from other parents. Beth's experience as an educator also gave her an advantage. She was well equipped to help her daughter. Beth now had a plan to get Karlye set up for success, in the best possible way.

Karlye's parents fought to the nail, and when she was two years old, they were able to get her into the center-based *applied behavior analysis (ABA)* program at California State University, Fresno (CSUF). Beth had attended a seminar called, Autism Perspectives. It was there that she heard Dr. Amanda Nicolson speak. Beth was incredibly inspired! "I have a hard time sitting through seminars like that….but Dr. N gave me hope," she said. This was the motivation behind getting Karlye into the ABA center at the CSUF, which Dr. Nicolson was the clinical director of.

Karlye's father and Beth still maintained different philosophies on how to help their daughter. Beth said, "He was more of the one who thought she would just grow out of it in time, but I was more of the realist." Beth believed that they had to plan for the different possibilities of Karlye's future. According to Beth, Karlye's father saw it as unnecessary planning. That made things difficult. Soon after they dove deep into the autism community, Karly's parents would split up. This made everything incredibly challenging. I can imagine how difficult that was for Beth.

Beth's attendance at meetings and dedicated involvement, diminished tremendously. There were policy and administration changes happening simultaneously at the ABA center, and Beth felt it. She no longer enjoyed the support meetings there. Beth rarely heard any celebrations at the meetings. In fact, she was scared to death hearing all the negative possibilities. "I can't live on the negative side of it. I *have* to see the positive," Beth explained. She stopped feeling like she could really relate to the other parents there; parents of boys, or those dealing with aggressive behaviors in their children. Beth felt like an outsider to some extent. She was a mother of a daughter with autism, a separation from her spouse underway, and little support elsewhere.

Being A Single Special Needs Mom

After the separation was final and Beth was a newly single mother, her life got more challenging. Beth's mother was the one person that could help out with Karlye. knowing this, you might imagine how difficult it must've been for the girls, when Beth's mom moved out of state. Sometimes, out of pure desperation, to help manage Karlye's meltdowns, Beth would have to ask her ex-husband to step in momentarily on her days with their daughter. However, Beth often felt like she couldn't really depend on him for Karlye.

Beth believes the autism related issues were about 70 percent the cause of her divorce. There were other issues too. However Beth feels autism played a huge role.

Karlye has two half brothers from her father, but they are not in her life. This limits the amount of support available to Beth for Karlye. Beth is sometimes torn between looking at Karlye's future and planning for it, versus not wanting to look that far ahead. It's a painful thought that includes inescapable loneliness for her daughter. Some friends encourage Beth to take it one day at a time, but Beth doesn't completely agree. She knows she has to have a plan for Karlye, especially as a single mom with minimal help.

As a single mother it's difficult when Beth needs to talk to someone. She wrestles with the need to talk about Karlye's autism, and not wanting to leave a friend with a heavy heart. "I don't want them to feel bad for me. I don't feel bad for me," Beth says. There's also times when Beth admittedly needs a break! She loves her daughter but some adult time is essential (well for every adult person) and Beth is no exception to that.

There was a time Beth recalls when she was at the lake with friends. In the forefront of her mind, Karlye was there, she's always there. She could have looked at all the fun activities that everyone was enjoying, and really felt bad about the "my child *should* be doing this" intrusive thoughts. Instead, when her friend started to ask about Karlye, Beth was hesitant and held back from diving into that conversation. Her friend quickly realized, and changed the topic of the conversation.

As I've said before, sometimes we can get deeply lost in raising our children, especially raising children with special needs. We can get so lost that we forget to breathe. We forget to look in the mirror, or take a shower for that matter. Sometimes Beth gives herself permission to remember Beth. It was a brutal reminder to me, about the importance of the balance between self-care and caring for someone other than myself. It's like that saying goes, "you must first help yourself before you can help others".

People tell Beth that she's not alone because she has Karlye. This is true and Beth enjoys hanging out with her daughter, but she still needs self-care and support. "I envy you parents that have help or someone," Beth disclosed about how she sometimes feels. She has Karlye for twenty-three days a month, and it's 24 hour supervision of Karlye during that time.

Beth remained in contact with some of the autism parents she had met at the ABA center when Karlye was little. Sometimes jokes are exchanged between a few of the single moms. They joking say they're ready to send their children "off to dad's" for the weekend. There is some truth to that, as Beth confirmed by saying "I need a mom break sometimes, a movie, some cuss words, and adult moments."

The single parent jokes are all in good fun, but really, when you have a partner in the home, parents are often able to take shifts. This makes it possible to not have to do it ALL on your own. You can make a meeting, find time for self-care, or go to the grocery store without your special-needs child. Even if it's not a whole lot of time, when you have a two-parent home, a close relative, or a friend to take on that role of supporter, you get those moments. Beth, like many women raising children on their own, is not easily afforded that luxury. That personal time is especially helpful and vital, when you're managing stress or meltdowns for that matter!

Karlye's Meltdowns, Having to Call in the Calvary

As Beth explained, Karlye didn't have very aggressive behaviors. She didn't kick, bite, or anything like that. She would grab your arm and squeeze if she was upset. Most of her meltdowns have consisted of having a tantrum on the floor. The fact is, it's much easier to remove a flailing three-year-old from some place, rather than a lanky, dead weight, upset, eleven-year-old. As much as she didn't want to, Beth would call Karlye's father to help out in those instances — which have notably not been many.

During Christmas time, back when Karlye was around seven years old, Beth was preparing her for a trip to the store. They were going to get items for Grandma's salami tray. It was supposed to be a quick in-and-out stop, but it took a little longer than expected. Oh no! I can guess what happened next, can you?

Karly had enough! She dropped to the floor, laying there; kicking, screaming, and crying. Just as I suspected! An older lady came over to them, waving her finger at Karlye's face. She started telling Karlye that Santa wasn't gonna come to her house that night, because of how she was "acting". This was not taken lightly by Beth. Without hesitation, Beth grabbed that lady's swaggering finger and said, "you need to walk away right now!" The women proceeded to say that she understood. It was obvious she didn't have a clue. Beth responded with, "my daughter's Autistic, she doesn't understand…and if she does, imagine what she's thinking in her head right now, that Santa's not gonna

111

come to her house now…walk away, and walk away quickly, because I don't have the patience for it!"

The manager came over to the scene after a while. Karlye was still on the floor. He told Beth they needed to leave the store. Beth assured him that if Karlye wasn't too heavy to carry, they would've been long gone! Not too happy about calling Karlye's father, Beth needed to employ his help. Karlye was dead weight on the floor. Beth added, "it's my fault, I took her shopping too long, but don't we all make mistakes?" It's true, we all make mistakes as parents, and we learn by the repercussions from our different kids, like Karlye. It's easy to forget the magnitude of the repercussions as well. Sometimes, you end up paying for pushing the envelope. Can you blame Beth for trying to accomplish this seemingly small task with Karlye? Beth didn't like having to call in the "calvary" for support, but it was one of those moments of necessity.

Karlye's Appendicitis

Looking back to shortly after her separation, Beth got into a routine. On the days Karlye's father was scheduled to have her, Beth would wake Karlye up early in the morning, get her in the car and drop her off with him. One particular day, when Karly was around five years old, she was stiff as a board getting into the car. She wouldn't bend her legs or move her body. Every bell and whistle went off for Beth! She instinctively knew that something was very wrong. Karlye was extremely ill.

Karlye was taken to the hospital. She was septic! For doctors to administer antibiotics, they had to run a *PICC line* for several days. The doctors couldn't even perform surgery because of how sick she was. She could have died on the table. How terrifying!

Karlye's father tried to be there in his own way. It was a tough situation already, and being separated made everything a little more awkward. Beth felt like her ex-husband was monitoring her care of their daughter, and it was frustrating for Beth. She was 100 percent, solely dedicated to the care of her daughter, and wasn't interested in any mediocre drama.

Remember how Karlye has autism and is nonverbal? Well the nurses at the hospital would ask Karlye how she was feeling, expecting a response each check-in, for the entire five days they had been there! They were informed of her condition, and it was in the charts. "She's not going to answer you no matter haw many times you ask her," Beth wanted to scream at the nurses! The nurses continued probing Karlye, waiting for her answers, with questions they asked her like "Does this hurt", or "Do you feel hot? Do you want to do something?" Beth wanted to make a giant poster to hang over Karlye's bed saying, "My Child is Autistic and Nonverbal"! Maybe that would give 'em a clue.

The manner in which the team would come in to check on five-year-old Karlye, was another frustration for Beth. They were loud and didn't seem to comprehend the fact that this child with autism, had sensory

114

difficulties as well, which again was in the charts. Beth said it was as if the nurses were "screaming at her!" "If you want to hear someone scream, keep doing that, she'll be screaming, and when that starts, Im gonna walk out, and let you deal with it," Beth recalled thinking. It is no secret that this situation brought out the "mama bear" in Beth.

When people don't understand the complexity of autism, it's frustrating. Add first responders, nurses, or doctors to that list, and it can make any medical emergency a real nightmare for our kids, and us special-needs parents too! At times like that, it makes you think — community awareness and support would be amazing.

Sometimes the Closest Supports Still "Don't Get It"

Grandma

Though her autism journey has been mostly alone, there have been a few supports that have come through for Beth and Karlye. The problem is that even when they mean well, they still don't fully understand Karlye and her personality with autism. It's common for many to claim they have a great understanding of autism, but often they don't. Their actual understanding of the condition is rather limited.

When Beth's mother lived in the same city, she would help with Karlye when she could. "She didn't really get it," Beth said, regarding her mother's understanding of Karlye's autism. For example, when giving Karlye a cookie, it has to be round, and look complete. She'll meltdown if it's the wrong shape or broken. When Beth tries to explain this to her mom, it is interpreted as Karlye being spoiled. Grandma likes doing things her way. Her parenting "expertise" is offended when Beth tries to teach her different approaches, specific to Karlye. Beth believes that there are bigger, more important battles to fight. She said that she is willing to, "cut cheese in skinny cubes, find the round cookie in the box," to avoid those battles with Karlye altogether. It is a real power struggle. If it isn't Karlye's way, she might fling that plate of cheese at you.

Beth simply wants her mom to understand that when she tells her not to do something a certain way, it's not because she's upset with her mother. It just needs to be Karlye's way in those instances. Grandma loves both Beth and Karlye, and they reciprocate the feeling, but adhering to Beth's request has not been easy for her mom.

Step Grandma

One summer, Beth's stepmom invited her and Karlye over for a swim, and they accepted the invite. Karlye enjoys swimming. Beth thought it might be a good idea.

As mentioned, sometimes those who intend to do well, end up triggering issues unintentionally. This was exactly one of those situations. In an enjoyable social setting, Karlye needs time to warm up. She'll take that time to decide what she likes, and what she doesn't like. When she's ready she'll come to you. If she's pressured, or not given the time, it won't result in a good situation.

117

While they were in the pool, Beth recalls her stepmom saying, "Karlye get the noodle… Karlye look at the water fall…", and it didn't stop there! Beth's stepmom continued with, "Karlye look…Karlye come… Karlye go". Beth could see Karly escalating there in the water. When Karlye escalates, she begins to stand on her "tippy toes". She starts to look as if she had a 5 hour energy drink! She started to do a little jog in place, which Beth could clearly see happening. Her stepmom didn't seem to catch it. This visit was supposed to be fun for Karlye, but it quickly caused her to feel very unhappy and frustrated. Inevitably the visit was cut short.

Situations like this are very difficult for Beth. She doesn't want to insult the person who is trying their hardest to engage with her child. I admire that about Beth. I know more people that wouldn't try, than would!

In situations like that at step grandma's, Beth wonders if she should let them figure it out on their own, or correct them. She also never wants to make others feel uncomfortable because of her daughter.

So, Beth accepts invitations as opportunities to socialize. She says she won't know unless she tries. There are still many situations in which Beth can almost guarantee the outcome. She chooses for her and Karly not to attend those functions, which likely will end badly.

Please Don't Feel Uncomfortable

When Beth declines invites to events and functions, it's not because of the typical fear that resides within the minds of many special-needs parents. It's due to not wanting other's to feel uncomfortable with her daughter's autism. For example, when she and Karlye get invited to watch her nephew play baseball, she believes that the attention should be on her nephew. She knows that Karlye may behave in ways, making disruptive sounds, possibly screaming and making movements that draw attention. It would take the focus off of her nephew, and on managing Karlye's behaviors. Despite the possible outcomes, Karlye has never had an outrageous meltdown with close family. Still, Beth dreads her family feeling uncomfortable, and getting embarrassed. For this reason she declines invites to those types of funcitons. She's not even sure if her family truly understands her rationale.

Beth's Grandfather

As a small child, Beth has memories of her own grandfather with special needs. He was wheelchair bound. Her grandmother would wheel him outside, so that he could sit and relax under a tree. It was always uncomfortable for Beth when he was around. He was a big, rough man, confined to a chair. The chair was bulky and awkward. Beth always felt like he was staring at her when they'd sit at the dinner table. She remembers that feeling. Before having Karlye, Beth admits that she was somewhat uncomfortable in an environment where someone with special needs was. She didn't know how to behave or what to do.

The possibility of someone feeling uncomfortable in a room with Karly, is one of Beth's biggest "problems" with autism. "In fact, I go out of my way to be consciously aware to know where she's at and what she needs," Beth said. Almost as if to avoid any impositions on others. This requires having the right activities and reinforcers on hand at all times. It's really an effort of consideration for others on Beth's part. It's her way of doing the right thing for everyone.

In sharing about her grandfather, and being uncomfortable around him as a child, Beth remembered another situation that happened at school with Karlye. Interestingly, Karlye's fellow students were quite comfortable with her, while their parents were obviously not.

A Memorable Special Event.

When Karlye was in the second grade, a few girls took interest in her. Mornings had been challenging for Karlye, which sometimes resulted in her having meltdowns at school. One little girl in particular, would ask her teacher if she could try to help out. The young girl and her friends, were somewhat buddies with

Karlye. Beth was very moved by such a young person making such a big gesture of kindness toward her daughter.

At that year's Christmas program, Karlye was having a hard time. When Karlye is done with school, she is...done! This was the case for Karlye. Her school day was done. She was ready to be home and stay home, and she ended up back at school later that evening for her Christmas program. Remember, many children with autism thrive on routine, and when changes occur, it can be the perfect recipe for a meltdown.

As a special-needs parent, inclusion is often a fight in public education. Even though it was tremendously difficult for Beth (managing Karlye's routine disruption repercussions) she felt that her daughter *needed* to have this experience. This was an opportunity for Karlye to be included in her school's Christmas program with *neurotypical* students.

When Karlye's class was up on stage, she was still having a hard time. It just so happened that the one little girl who became Karlye's unofficial "helper", along with her two friends, stopped singing during their performance. They were trying to help Karlye by encouraging her to participate. Beth said she could hear the girls cheering, "Come on Karlye!" Beth was overwhelmed with emotion by this. However, the looks on their parents' faces, didn't share the same disposition.

Come to find out later, the parents blamed Karlye for ruining their daughters' Christmas program, according to what the teacher told Beth. Those parents had stopped recording and taking pictures of their daughters all in their pretty dresses, with giant red bows in their hair, while they helped Karlye. Beth felt that the parents should have been more encouraging and even proud about their daughters' showing amazing character. What was recorded of their children might have not been perfect, but if they looked closely they had a glimpse of true humanitarianism. Even if their parents' couldn't see it, the character displayed by those girls, "it means the world to me, and it means the world to Karlye,"

Beth said.

After disturbing Karlye's routine, in order for her to participate in that Christmas program, she had a major meltdown. This meltdown with tears, lasted approximately 45 minutes. She was exhausted! All of which Karlye and her mom endured, the other parents had no understanding of. How incredibly unfair that must have felt!

Beth picked up her daughter and carried her to the car. Then, she sat and cried her eyes out too. She experienced the emotional turmoil of the entire ordeal with Karlye. Special-needs parents, inevitably do in situations like that. Sometimes it seems like nothing is fair when looking at the past, present, or even the future, for our differently-abled kiddos.

The Future

It's difficult for Beth to think about the future for her daughter as mentioned before. At the expense of sounding morbid, Beth shared that she sometimes thought it would be better if Karlye and her left this world at the same time. Not to be confused with any intrusive death wishes. Beth simply gave this example to express the magnitude of her not wanting Karly to be left behind, by herself after Beth leaves this world. Beth fears that Karlye will have no one truly looking out for her.

Beth feels that Karlye's half brothers would maybe only minimally tend to arrangements of putting Karlye in a facility. Her father's health makes it unlikely for him to be in a position to care for her, should anything happen to Beth. The statistics of special-needs women being abused and raped in living facilities, is extraordinary high as well. It is this bleak future that Beth fears. Beth has to plan for Karlye's future, although she'd rather not. This is one of the hardest things to process for her. It's a truly uncomfortable responsibility to take on; planning the care of your vulnerable child, for when you are no longer around.

The topic of Karlye's future brings up painful thoughts for Beth. She wonders about the things her daughter is going to miss; first date, prom, wedding day, walking her down the aisle. This is the reality for Beth, since her daughter's developmental gaps are now more evident, compared to when she was younger. "You can dream, and think about those things when she was little, because you didn't know the future…, but now I know, she's gonna live with me," Beth says. So, Beth tries to do the best for Karlye now as she prepares for her daughter's future. She continues to stay proactive, and is continually learning how to navigate a life with autism.

It's Not The World Against Autism

Being a school teacher, Beth walks a fine line. She mentioned that some kids behave in ways that warrant expulsion or suspension, even some with autism. This is extremely case by case. She has parents that she has to explain this to, and the parents do not know that Beth herself is a parent of an Autistic child. Beth has encountered parents who think the teacher is "out to get their Autistic child". She's a bit upset by this.

On the other hand, as a parent of a child with autism, Beth is more keen to notice certain nuances in children. She can see when a child is in distress, and feels inclined to go over and try to help the situation. Other teachers have made comments, indicating that they see Beth as wanting to label every student as having "autism". Beth says, "the school always sees me like, oh God, there she goes! I see a kid having a moment, and they get mad at me because I go and try to help with my fuzzy pen or stickers." Beth tries to help the student calm down in those situations. "You can discipline him or her after," Beth says.

Beth feels that she's just helping those kids. She would do the same whether they had a disability or not. She does admit that she can see the tendencies a mile away. Many parents of children with autism that I've encountered, can relate to this, including myself!

Family Impact

Autism has definitely had an impact in all areas of Beth's life. "I think I've isolated myself from my family, events, baseball games, stuff I would have definitely been at," Beth says. It's a different kind of life for sure. Beth talked about the considerations made for celebrating Mother's Day and Father's Day. Going to Batter up Pancakes on Father's Day, when there are a hundred people in there on a Saturday, is likely not going to happen. For Mother's Day, special plans have to be made as well. Beth will take her mom on Saturday, on a weekend Karlye is at her dad's, and everyone else can go do Mother's Day brunch on Sunday. Beth knows Karlye would have a difficult time in social settings like these, where waiting is required.

There has been a definite rescheduling of a lot of things that make it more suited to Karlye's needs. Beth says, "If we're at somebody's house it's not a problem, but there's no more Sunday brunch at the country club." She pointed out, if Karlye's father doesn't remember that when planning, " he ends up out in the car with Karlye on her iPad…and they bring his plate out." Definite adaptations and modifications have been made for both

Karlye and her parents, to participate in family functions. Karlye's autism has changed Beth's world.

Beth's Perspective on Autism: Karlye's Happy Bubble

Beth refers to 90 percent of Karlye's autism as, Karlye's "happy bubble". Autism lets her live in that "happy bubble". Beth says, "but when that 10 percent hits, like get out of the way!"

Karlye's autism allows her to not have the same concerns that keep other people up at night. In Beth's journey with autism, she has seen adults be more judgmental than kids! For example, when Karlye's in her "happy bubble", running, squealing and screeching at the park, it's not the other children who are giving her funny stares.

Autism is all controlling. It captures Beth's entire day. She can be at work and starts thinking about where Karlye is in her day. First at school, then at the autism center, and so on.

Everything has to be prompted. Even saying "hello" or "goodbye" has a script. Prompting and routines are life. Watch out, you don't want to miss a step, that's for sure!

Autism for Karlye, means living in her own world. Beth says, "I mean its not just her autism, its my autism. Maybe I live it more than she does, because she doesn't know what else is out there." Even though Beth feels the sadness, stress, and gets exhausted, Karlye doesn't feel it, or live it the way Beth does. "She's just happy," Beth said.

Beth's Message for Other Parents

Beth says that if she could go back in time, she would have tried more things when Karlye was younger. She suggests to try participating in more events while they're younger, since kids are more manageable physically. When they're crying, you can just pick them up and it's not awkward in public. She also says that she would have pushed the envelope more. She'd take

Karlye to more places, like restaurants and more movie theaters.

"I would say to try to get them to as many places instead of being closed off," Beth said. She continued, "I think from when Karlye was between two to four years old, I was more angry and resentful, and just closed off as a whole." At the beginning of Beth's journey with autism, one of her biggest concerns she said was, "wondering how my child was going to fit into society." "I don't think I tried enough, I think I isolated us, plus I was going through a divorce," she said. In recognizing what she thinks she could have done differently, Beth is able to offer this advice to other parents. Managing autism has been quite the challenge for her.

To Cure or Not to Cure?

If there was a way to get rid of Karlye's autism today, Beth would do it. She agrees that it would be a multilayered decision, should a cure for autism exist. It would be tough after investing the last near decade to accommodating Karlye's autism, and knowing her to be the person she is. Beth says she would say "yes" because she would want her daughter to flourish, and not struggle as much. She believes academics would be extremely difficult to catch up on, but at least her daughter would be socially accepted. Since no cure exists, Beth has let Karlye's autism show her the way, and it has taught her a great deal overall.

Autism the Teacher

Beth shared that she is not a very tolerant, nor patient person, but autism has helped her calm that part about herself. Through her journey with autism, Beth has sat back and learned to see her daughter as a precious gift. The reality of autism has encouraged her to reflect on life's meaning, and her relationship with God has grown by "100 percent, probably 150 percent," Beth said. Beth says that if she was single the rest of her life, she'd probably be okay with it, as she's got a lifelong commitment with Karlye. Autism has shown Beth a capacity to love that is beyond comparison.

Autism Can be very different, and yet very similar for those raising children with the condition. I can personally relate to the last statement Beth shared. She said, "I have never loved so hard in my life."

My Take

Beth's story is one for all the single autism mothers out there. I'm awestruck at how she's managed through much of her autism journey independently! She touched on some topics that not everyone likes to talk about. For example, Beth shared about her decision to look optimistically at her daughter's future, despite the challenges that it brings. It's true, we autism moms sometimes jokingly say that "we have to live forever". At the root of it though, is a fear. This is a fear of leaving our vulnerable children behind when we are gone from this world. Beth worries about what that future will be like for her daughter Karlye. It is not easy, but she makes a strong point. While it's healthy to take things one day at a time, planning for the future is important! I realize how blessed I am to have a large family. I know that my kids will be there for each other when their father and I are not able to. Not everyone is afforded this reality.

The part of this story where autism is thrown into Beth's life, and she gives up her prior expectations, is powerful! To see her child lose skills, I couldn't even imagine that. Then growing a new perspective and seeing the joy her daughter is filled with, is amazing. It brought a smile to my face when she described Karlye's "happy bubble".

I nodded along when she talked about the people who try to be supportive, but it ends up not being helpful for Karlye. Can't we all just find the round cookie in the box, and all is well in the world? Beth gives an example of graciously accepting help and being optimistic, even when it doesn't pan out.

I am inspired by the strength that Beth possesses. The courage she has to co-parent as a divorcee is inspiring as well. Her ability to be open about longing to have a moment without autism, is incredibly honest. This reminds me that we are human, and we need to take care of ourselves too. This leads to the topic of self-care, which she brings to the table. That is huge! We can't help anyone if we can't first help ourselves, right? I believe its critical to be healthy to take care of our children with special needs, and sometimes we need adult time, single or not.

Like she said, "I have never loved so hard," I know the very feeling! The thing that is the most inspiring to me about Beth's story, is her immense growth in faith. I cannot imagine this special-needs journey, without my own faith in God.

CHAPTER 5

Lucky One

Bernadette is a childhood friend I grew up with. We went to the same schools, and had some of the same friends. We ran into each other again in college and now stay in touch through social media. I noticed that she started posting autism related memes and photos of her son about a year ago. I reached out to Bernadette and asked if she'd like to share her story with me. She was a little hesitant at first. She ultimately agreed and invited me to her house to be interviewed.

Bernadette is a mom of four boys. Her oldest son is thirteen years old, and her youngest is four years old. Her "bookends" as she referred to them, have been diagnosed with *autism spectrum disorder (ASD)*.

Although Bernadette's oldest son is severely affected by ASD, she wanted to focus more on telling me her story with her youngest son, Nicholas. Her experience with her oldest son was quite the challenge.

First Meeting With Autism

Bernadette, very similar to myself, didn't know anyone with autism or any special needs for that matter, before she encountered the condition in her first born. She says that he was different from the start. Being a first-time mother thirteen years ago, everything was new for her. She chalked up a lot of her son's peculiarities to not having other babies around him, being her first child, and the first grand baby of the family.

She was trusting of her pediatrician, who met her and baby with a smile at every visit. When she felt the questions pertaining to her son's development rising up in her gut, the trust in the doctor started to weaken. Bernadette, like many of us moms, had a hunch that things weren't quite right with her son. "I knew he was different..pretty much from day one," she said.

Despite her suspicions, she was protective and defensive when it came to her baby boy. As he grew, she started to see more signs of autism in him. All she knew of the condition was that it was "bad". She refused the idea.

When her oldest son was not yet three years old, Bernadette remembers a specific incident. Her brother and sister-in-law were visiting from out of town. Her sister-in-law proceeded to question her son's development, as he was not yet talking at that time. She suggested maybe having him screened for ASD. Bernadette remembers quickly responding with, "no, that's not what's going on, he doesn't have that." However, Bernadette knew deep down that something wasn't right, and she was determined to get to the bottom of it.

The Long Journey She Remembers

Her oldest son did end up getting diagnosed with *autism spectrum disorder (ASD)* on his third birthday. The assessment was done through the *Central Valley Regional Center (CVRC)*. Bernadette learned to advocate and fight for her son to receive intervention services in private clinical settings, and in public education. She underwent her own emotional challenges in facing everything. Bernadette became a mother who is a beacon for many. She is a strong advocate, and says, "I continue to learn, I'm constantly learning, and applying." Bernadette learned to think outside the box in navigating a life with special needs, with her oldest son. This would give her a leg up for what was in store a few years later.

Hand Me Down Genes

As her family grew, Bernadette paid special attention to her boys' development. She said, "I would kind of do my own little check-in. I wanted to make sure I didn't miss anything." She also admits that she saw some autism tendencies in her second and third sons. "They had some symptoms, and so I had them informally screened," Bernadette said. Those little traits that she identified in her other two boys, were just a little bit problematic. Her second oldest had difficulties with understanding social norms. "He wasn't real good at keeping appropriate distance from people, and he was loud," she explained. Big brother already had tools in place, which Bernadette made part of the daily routine for everyone. "I think using the things we already had, just helped in a big way, " she said. Her third born son had more sensory type issues. Bernadette explained that this little guy was selective when it came to food and clothing. " Shoot, there were days were we couldn't leave the house because the seams on his socks weren't lined up just right," she giggled a little. Bernadette's family, like many of our autism families, went through a season of only chicken nuggets and fries.

Bernadette worked tirelessly with all of her boys, while she was pregnant with her last baby. She started to see a silver lining in her oldest son's condition. She had established supports in her home, and generally in her life already. It wasn't like walking through the woods in the dark anymore. It was the new way of life. It was their "normal".

Lucky Baby

On a warm June morning in 2016, at 10:25am, the newest member of the family arrived. Nicholas was born. Bernadette says, "I knew I was having a boy, but I still couldn't believe it." There was something particular and fascinating about this little guy, Bernadette explained. Fascinating for sure, Nicholas was born *en caul.* He was born within an intact amniotic sack. This phenomena is said to happen in every 1 in 80,0000 births. In some cultures, this type of birth signifies luck. As they would have it, Nicholas was a "lucky baby"

During her pregnancy with Nicholas, everything went relatively smoothly. Bernadette kept all of her routine appointments as scheduled. Every ultrasound was an exciting moment for her. "I was really kinda trying to convince myself that maybe they got it wrong and we were finally getting our girl." Having a boy, nonetheless, she was happy with the idea of her four boys growing together, and becoming strong young men some day. Bernadette excitedly anticipated the future. She was happy knowing her oldest son would have three brothers to support him throughout his life.

Bringing Baby Home

It was time for baby Nicholas to go home, and meet brothers. Bernadette couldn't wait, and neither could the boys.

Though her oldest son didn't seem to pay much attention to the new baby, he'd "side-eye" the bundle whenever he heard his little cries. Bernadette's other two boys were over the moon about their new baby. "They wanted to help, to hold Nicholas, and you better believe they made sure your hands were washed if you were gonna touch their baby," Bernadette said, (and we laughed at the cuteness).

Nicholas wasn't a fussy baby. He was the only one of Bernadette's children that took to sleeping in a crib pretty quickly. Bernadette explained how Nicholas was cuddly and would just melt into her arms. He had a head full of hair. "It just kept growing," she added, haha! Bernadette remembers her own hair growing and going wavy during her pregnancy with him as well. There were definitely unique things associated with baby Nicholas that Bernadette recognized. She even though at one point, "are these things signs of some sort?"

Happy Nicholas

Nicholas was a happy baby. He was thriving. Milestones were being met on time. Bernadette felt less stressed about the potential of her youngest son having a condition like his older brother now. Nicholas was crawling, self-feeding, sitting up, playing peek-a-boo, among other normal developments. He was making eye contact and babbling as well. These were all things that his oldest brother didn't do with ease, or at all, as a baby. A sense of relief came over Bernadette.

When Nicholas was around six months old Bernadette shared that he was "a happy morning baby." She says that Nicholas would pull himself up to a standing position in his crib every morning. He'd look over and give her the biggest smile. "It was our little morning routine," she said. "He was so cute with his wild hair everywhere, and the biggest cheesy smile on his chubby little face, just waiting for me to smile back," she said.

Nicholas continued growing and thriving. It wasn't long before he started walking. He seemed pretty quick with some of his development, however, his articulation was just a little slow. That didn't worry Bernadette too much at first. However, she started to notice some things when he was almost almost two years old.

The sweet happy toddler was gentle. He was all smiles most of the time, and enjoyed exploring. Nicholas loved to play with toy cars and blocks. He would make paths, and line up those toys almost strategically. His older brother didn't do much of that, although it's common for children with autism -lining up things that is. Bernadette said, "I thought it was fine, because he was reaching all his milestones, and lining up things is somethings a lot of little kids do." Then Bernadette noticed something while Nicholas was playing with his blocks. His brother decided he wanted to borrow a block for what he was building. In little brother's defense, he wasn't asked. This resulted in Nicholas having a major tantrum.

The longer Bernadette witnessed the tantrum she knew it wasn't just a tantrum. It was a meltdown! Nicholas couldn't help himself. He was flailing on the ground, he couldn't formulate his words. He was yelling, kicking, banging his head subtly against the floor where he was laying. No other toy would suffice. Bernadette remembered the sinking feeling in her gut.

Tantrums VS Meltdowns

Often times when an Autistic child has a *meltdown,* it is confused with a *tantrum.*

The two can look very much alike, however, they are not the same. The difference is that tantrums usually occur as an attempt to control a situation or to obtain something desired, that is unattainable in that moment. A meltdown on the other hand, is a physical emotional response to a situation; usually one that is overwhelming in nature.

Nicholas started having more and more meltdowns. His triggers mostly surrounded an interruption in routine, and play. Bernadette started to watch Nicholas like a hawk, now wondering if he too was Autistic like his older brother. If he was, this would be brand new for the family, as his symptoms were very different than the autism the family was already accustomed to.

Other Signs and Symptoms

Nicholas was verbal, but he started stuttering. His thoughts seemed bigger than what he could express. Bernadette reached out to a *speech language pathologist (SLP)* that had worked with her oldest son. Bernadette was assured that this was normal for kids Nicholas's age. Sure enough, soon after that conversation with the SLP, his words started catching up to his thoughts.

Bernadette says, "Nicholas is extremely bright!" The social piece, and his self injurious behaviors, were the concerning behaviors he had. Her oldest son didn't display aggressive behaviors at that age, but had developed some around the same time that concerns about Nicholas surfaced. She wondered if maybe some of it was learned behavior. "Initially I waited to look into it further, because my oldest son now engages in some *self-injurious behaviors (SIB)*. I wasn't sure if Nicholas was mimicking what he saw," Bernadette said. However, she explained that the behaviors looked a little too different for that to be the case.

Was it Autism?

Bernadette was a bit nervous about having her youngest son screened for autism. She also knew the importance of early intervention, and Nicholas's third birthday was approaching. She decided to have a referral made for him to be clinically evaluated. Here she was now having to accept the possibility that another one of her boys was Autistic. What would life be like with two boys on the spectrum? Perhaps it wouldn't be too different since autism was already in the mix.

The Diagnosis

This time Bernadette did things a little bit differently than she did with her oldest son. "We were able to take a back door approach," she said. The therapy center that her oldest son was attending at that time, had a clinical psychologist on site doing assessments for autism. In this manner, they were able to bypass waiting for a referral from the pediatrician to CVRC. The diagnosis was made by the clinical psychologist at the ABA center, then forwarded to the pediatrician who was able to apply the proper insurance codes for the diagnosis, in order for Nicholas to begin receiving services. Nicholas was given the diagnosis of *autism spectrum disorder (ASD)*.

Acceptance Again

you might think because she already was a veteran autism mom, that this diagnosis might have been a piece of cake. It was not. Bernadette said, "I recognized the signs, but I actually dreaded seeing those words on paper….*autism spectrum disorder*." She also remembers telling Nicholas's dad that she "didn't want this for him." She didn't want autism for him, she just wanted him to be a happy "normal" little boy. She knew she couldn't escape the reality. "Autism is kind of like death and taxes," she sighed. It's one of those things in life that when it happens, there's no escaping it.

Starting Services

When Bernadette's oldest son started receiving therapy at three years old, there were some incredible one's available. There weren't many options, however. Now eight years later, it seemed as though there were better programs available for Nicholas. Perhaps a combination of better service options, and just being seasoned a bit in navigating the journey with autism made resources seem more available. Either way, Bernadette noticed the difference. It was bitter sweet.

This time around, as compared to big brother's experience, ABA services were started earlier, and more efficiently. Bernadette felt that Nicholas would have a different experience because his autism affects him differently than his older brother's. She said, "frankly, we're 'better at autism', as my six year old likes to say." Straight from the mouths of babes!

First Day of ABA

Nicholas's first day of ABA brought up a lot of emotions for this mom. He was excited to start his "new school," Bernadette remembered. She on the other hand, was a nervous wreck. She felt guilty for sending her baby off into the big world of ABA at three years old.

The night before his first day of ABA, Bernadette made a run to the grocery store, and took Nicholas with her. She asked me, "you ever have those moments when you look at your kids, and feel like you're seeing them for the first time?" She went on to add, "I had one of those moments. I was completely undistracted, and could see his handsome little face." I couldn't help but smile as she explained, because the truth was, I've had many of those moments.

You can get so busy and distracted with the hustle and bustle of everyday life, that you don't always focus on the beautiful subtle things like those moments. Then you when you have a chance to appreciate the details; the curves of little cheeks, little lips moving as they speak, it can actually take your breath away. I absolutely knew what Bernadette was talking about. She couldn't resist adding, "and ugh, those lashes again, when my little guy was looking right at me." I smiled at that too. The guilt came over her in that moment at the store. She realized then that she had been somewhat distracted with so much life running through the halls of her home. Bernadette said, "my heart was glowing with love for this little human, in that moment as well." When they got home that evening, Nicholas helped pack his Batman backpack for the next day.

More Mom Guilt!

The following morning, Bernadette took Nicholas to his new ABA center. She explained how he was a little shy when they arrived and entered the building. After a while, he made the transition to an area in the back where there were toys. The guilt of sending her three year old off to ABA therapy that day, coupled with the reality of his diagnosis, weighed on Bernadette. It had all reminded her of the experience of starting her oldest son in ABA, and all those encompassing thoughts. "I didn't want a life with schedules, work, and labels for my little guy now," she said. However, she wasn't as afraid of it for him, as she was with his older brother. She also was equipped with knowledge and knew the longterm benefits now.

He did well that first day, with only one lengthy meltdown. Bernadette said, " I felt really bad thinking he was missing his mommy. Then I learned, the meltdown was over a toy...go figure!" We both laughed at that one.

Now Nicholas has been receiving center-based ABA therapy for a little over a year. It's a bittersweet feeling for Bernadette, getting to see the benefits of starting a good quality program earlier than they did with big brother.

The Lessons Of Autism

Bernadette has experienced two flavors of autism. Her thirteen year old's more severe autism, has enriched her life in many ways. She is able to provide support and important information to other parents struggling in situations she was once in. Autism with her now four year old son Nicholas, has taught her new lessons. She has had to adopt new approaches with him. "Sometimes it's easy for me to forget that he's Autistic because of his language, and his age," she said. This is evident at times when Bernadette is trying to multitask, and Nicholas has something to tell his mom. She might be washing dishes and answering a question without looking at him. Then Nicholas will demand that she looks right at him before he continues. "I think it's funny and frustrating at the same time. He's learning about how you should look at the person you're speaking with, in ABA, which means I have to pause and look him right in the eyes.. then he'll finish his question or thought he wants to share," Bernadette laughed.

154

Overall Nicholas is doing well with ABA. He's still working on those meltdowns, and his language articulation. Bernadette is also learning to recognize the unique challenges and strengths associated with autism that are individual to each of her Autistic son's. "I feel like my bag of resources and tools has just expanded, and I feel way more confident," she said. She sees all of her sons as huge blessing and supports to each other.

Words for Other Parents

Bernadette emphasizes how *individual,* autism is. Even if you carry some of the same genes, have the same set of parents, or live in the same house, she says that autism can look very different within the same family. Her boys are a prime example of that. As a result, she feels it's important to take time to really get to know your kids. She advises parents to simply learn from the differences, but not to compare the success of one child to another's successes or failures. Bernadette encourages parents to build routines into their lives. These routines benefit everyone. She believes that just as autism is a whole family ordeal, routines and structure benefit the entire family. Finally, Bernadette urges parents to consciously slow down, take in the little moments. She says, "It's those moments where you feel like the lucky one."

My Take

I could relate to some of the experiences in this chapter. I too have four boys, with two on the autism spectrum. I love how Bernadette described the different "flavors" of autism regarding how different autism presented itself in her two boys.

A take away from this chapter, was that even though Bernadette had already been seasoned in autism, it was brand new for her with a different child. It's true that some people might think she wouldn't have the same emotional response as a "rookie" autism parent, but it was new again. Every autism experience is individual. It may have similarities, but can look completely different from one person to the next, even siblings. Also the guilt that she carried, and her not wanting her son to have autism, that was incredibly honest! Finally, she gives us a powerful reminder to slow down and appreciate our kiddos, autism and all! I agree that you become the "lucky one" when you learn do that.

CHAPTER 6

The Many Battles

We live in a digital age. Most of us spend more time on technology than in person with people. There are pros and cons to that. I like having access to community support at my fingertips. I have to say, in doing these interviews, I was given such a gift. I met a few parents in person for the first time. It's one thing to read their posts and see pictures, it's an entirely different experience, when you sit and hear their stories as they remember them. It's literally like reliving some of the parts with them. Chelsea is one of the moms I had the pleasure of meeting in person for the first time during our interview.

Chelsea and her husband have been married for a little over a decade. They live in their home with their only child, a little girl, named Chloe. Chloe was seven years old at the time of our interview.

Chloe has a*utism level III, sensory processing disorder (SPD), speech apraxia, attention deficit hyper-activity disorder (ADHD)* and is *nonverbal/preverbal.*

Brief History

Chelsea's parents were in their forties when they had her. Her father was working two jobs and playing baseball, so it literally left the the ladies together. Three ladies to be precise, Chelsea, her mom, and her grandmother, up until her grandmother's passing. The ladies were very close. They were like, "the three amigos," Chelsea said.

The teenage years were rough, but Chelsea's parents kept her grounded. Hard work and the value of keeping your word, are values Chelsea's parents instilled in their children.

Chelsea has a brother who is fifteen years older than her. It was more like being an only child a lot of the time with the age disparity. He was already an adult when Chelsea was a teenager. She says they get along fine, but they were closer when she was younger.

Chelsea's husband's name is Dwayne. He is in fact, an only child. Looks like Chelsea can relate to that. Dwayne is also a military veteran. The happy couple were only married for a year before they got pregnant.

Prior to becoming pregnant, Chelsea was diagnosed with the painful condition, *fibromyalgia*. "It was hell," she said. She had to learn how to manage the pain. Surprisingly during her pregnancy everything was great! Chelsea says the pain was non-existent during most of her pregnancy with her daughter. The final month of her pregnancy however, was extremely difficult. The painful symptoms of Chelsea's fibromyalgia started to creep up on her, along with the normal end of pregnancy discomforts. After Chloe was born, Chelsea felt ALL — the pain. It was as if the the pain had accumulated from those eight months prior of being absent, and hit her like a truck after the baby was born. Chelsea was juggling being a new mom, dealing with her condition, and still learning how to be a wife. Nonetheless, she was captivated with her new baby, which made it all worth it. Things seemed to be going well at home over the next year or so, but it wasn't long before Chelsea was blindsided, yet again. Her happy thriving daughter started to change.

Red Flags

Chloe was engulfed in both English and Spanish languages. She had nearly twenty-five words in both languages, but Chelsea said, "she brain dumped it all." She was developing typically, but then her language suddenly disappeared! About six months later, Chloe started stacking objects. Then everything became rigid. Change in anything was very difficult for Chloe, from changing clothes to eating different foods. Chloe was about two years old when all of this had surfaced. Chelsea however, started seeing these red flags in her daughter, since Chloe was a year old. Because of her young age at the time, Chelsea dismissed them.

There was one incident in particular that stood out to Chelsea, which wasn't as easily dismissed. The family was in the living room of their home. Chloe was playing with blocks, stacking them. She was standing in front of her parents, on the coffee table, and kept stacking. Then, little Chloe wanted her dad to pick her up, so she could continue to stack the blocks as close to the ceiling as possible. "That's not right," Chelsea said to her husband. She remembered her husband asking her to explain what he was doing wrong. Was he not picking his daughter up correctly? He wasn't aware that Chelsea was referring to their toddler's block stacking peculiarity.

In Chelsea's mind, it was completely normal for a toddler to stack blocks. The persistence, however, and need to have no interruption in stacking the blocks all the way to the ceiling, was not normal. Demanding another person to help her accomplish the task, that stood out to Chelsea as strange. Although her husband vaguely remembers that incident, it was a pivotal moment for Chelsea. Along with the loss of language Chloe experienced, this indicated to Chelsea that they needed to seek help.

Conflicting Thoughts on Assessments

Chelsea searched for an entire year to find someone to asses her daughter for developmental conditions. She even went against her husband's wishes at that time. He didn't believe anything was wrong with Chloe. Chloe's dad is an army veteran, which Chelsea feels made her husband more defensive. The thought that their daughter might have anything "wrong" with her, didn't sit well with him. He thought that maybe she just took after Chelsea's father; he was a late talker, did some head banging, and displayed symptoms similar to his granddaughter as a child. Chelsea disagreed. She was confident that having the level of language Chloe previously had, shouldn't just disappear without a good explanation.

Chelsea was persistent. She insisted that if they got Chloe assessed, and something was found, they would know what to do. If not, she was only two years old, so Chloe would have no recollection of the process. Chelsea thought, "what's the harm in finding out?"

Her husband then agreed to have their daughter assessed. Chelsea says that her husband didn't discourage her after that conversation, but she knew it was difficult for him to agree to. As the process went on, Chloe's father became more supportive.

The Evaluation

It was quite a process to get Chloe evaluated by the *Central Valley Regional Center (CVRC)*. Before that, the family had switched pediatricians three different times. While Chelsea was going to school to become a teacher, she had learned that families should be referred to their pediatricians, if any concerns arose, similar to what she was facing. At that time, there wasn't any available information about autism that Chelsea was aware of. All she knew was what she had learned in school — the pediatrician is the starting point. She eventually learned how different the actual navigation was surrounding special needs.

Chelsea had family that worked for the county. They suggested that getting Chloe behavioral health services would be helpful. As much as she hates to admit it, Chelsea didn't want to do that. She felt as if that was her last resort. Behavioral health was a scary name, and the journey was scary already, not knowing what to do, or where to go. It was terrifying for Chelsea. She remained determined to do whatever she needed to get answers, and to get her daughter the help she needed. Chloe was initially denied an assessment. Chelsea had to fight to have her daughter evaluated, and eventually she was. Finally, after waiting nearly five months, Chloe was assessed through CVRC.

Chelsea remembers finally getting the paperwork on Chloe's third birthday of all days. She went into the office to get her daughter's test results. There was a lot of paperwork that didn't all make sense, but the bottom line was that Chloe was diagnosed with autism spectrum disorder (ASD).

Some parents are relieved with receiving a diagnosis, and some are not. Chelsea was upset with these findings. She wanted to get out of the building and rush home to make sense of the report. After all the doctors appointments, jumping through hoops to get this assessment done, the results were finally in, and it wasn't what Chelsea wanted.

When Chelsea got home, she went through the report. It changes when, "you literally have those letters in black and white," she said. She clearly remembers the avalanche of emotions that came over her, in that moment. Chelsea sat and cried. She cried for an entire week! "I was a hermit for a week," she said.

After Chelsea had some time to let everything soak in, she decided to let her parents know about Chloe's diagnosis. She made a photo copy of the paperwork, and left it in their mailbox. When her parents read the paperwork, Chelsea's mom cried too. When her mother-in-law found out about the diagnosis, she was in disbelief.

A week of crying is all Chelsea allowed herself. Sometimes she wishes she gave herself more time to "morn". She was grieving for the loss of the child *without* a disability, she thought she'd have. This type of grief is experienced by many special-needs parents. You might find yourself riddled with guilt, after coming to a place of acceptance, and looking back at your season of, as I like to call it, "expectational morning".

Instead of wallowing in grief, Chelsea hit the ground running. Her husband had to be at work and she had to take matters into her own hands. There was no more time to sulk.

After Chloe was diagnosed with autism, she received the remainder of her diagnoses from several different doctors. At another medical clinic, Chloe was more recently diagnosed with ADHD. She had difficulties sitting still, eating meals, and generally focusing. It was a fight to get this assessment approved as well, due to Chloe being nonverbal. Chelsea persisted, instinctively knowing that ADHD was the only thing that made sense. This mom's instinct proved certain once again, and the diagnosis confirmed it. Another pediatric doctor determined that Chloe had *sensory processing disorder (SPD)*[4]. Also, Chloe's private speech providers confirmed that she had *speech apraxia*.

Change in Expectations

Chelsea never imagined her daughter would have all the diagnoses and challenges she does. From the time she was pregnant, Chelsea only ever wanted her daughter to be happy and successful. Both Chelsea and her husband struggled with math and reading as children. These seemed to be inherited difficulties, that Chelsea already anticipated her daughter would need help with. That part wasn't very different with her new diagnosis. Both of Chloe's parents wanted her to attend Catholic private school. It was now a matter of figuring out *how*, and *if*, that could happen as they had planned.

The Importance of Education for Chelsea

Education is very important to Chelsea. Growing up, her family didn't want her to struggle, having to work and go to school at the same time, like they did.

---

[4] Sensory processing disorder is a common condition among those with autism.

They didn't want her working in the fields. Her grandmother only attended public school for a very short period of time.

Education was pushed on Chelsea by her parents. Her grandmother instilled in her, that she needed to be successful in education to not be "stupid" like her, Chelsea said. Chelsea explained, "it's not like she was stupid, but English wasn't her first language." The message her grandma was trying to convey, is that education makes you, "smart".

Chelsea wanted her daughter to do well in school too. She knew her daughter might struggle in academics, but she wanted her to be happy and to make friends. That was until they were pitched the curveball of — autism. Autism changed ALL of that. Chelsea bluntly said, "that went down the shitter!" Their hopes and expectations changed, regarding education. How to teach Chloe, how to think outside of the box, and give her all the tools she needed to be successful, were top priorities now.

Everything was different and new with special needs in their lives now.

Getting Acquainted with Autism

Chelsea didn't know anyone with autism and had never been around it before her daughter's diagnosis. Autism was a brand new world for Chelsea, similar to my own experience. Since it was a foreign concept, Chelsea did what many mothers do and left no stone unturned. She again convinced her husband that it was better to rule things out with testing, especially while their daughter was young. This would make things more manageable and forgivable, Chelsea figured. She'd rather be proactive, instead of waiting it out and regretting not doing things earlier, years later.

Chelsea had genetic testing done for her daughter to rule out underlying conditions such as, *fragile x syndrome,* and *epilepsy,* among others. She also had tests such as, a *sleep study*, and an *electroencephalogram (EEG)* done on Chloe.

All results were inconclusive or negative. This meant that she didn't have any notable genetic markers linked to her autism.

From what she's learned, Chelsea believes that autism is a neurological condition that starts in the womb. She doesn't feel that her daughter was vaccine injured. She is a firm believer that the benefits of vaccines are important for her daughter's health.

Chelsea made it a point to learn everything she could on autism and the implications for her daughter. To avoid sounding ignorant, Chelsea made it a point to be prepared for all meetings and appointments, regarding her daughter. When it comes to fighting for her Chloe, Chelsea doesn't reserve her passion. She even shared that sometimes her language is somewhat uninhibited. I think a lot of us might be guilty of that, ha! Chelsea's religious affiliates, might be bigger fans of more reserved word choices, however.

Different Perspectives

When Chelsea was going through college, she had somewhat rebelled against the Catholic life she was engulfed in. Then, when she learned that her daughter had autism, she did a lot of praying in addition to research. Most of the time she prayed that she was wrong about things she knew instinctively to be true, regarding Chloe. "It was a lot of reading, a lot of caffeine, and sleepless nights, for multiple reasons," Chelsea said.

She was constantly adding to her knowledge base. Chelsea was absorbing new information from her college courses, to become a teacher, and from all of her research for Chloe.

Having a wealth of knowledge in education sometimes made things difficult for Chelsea, especially in her relationship with family. Sometimes she wished that she was still ignorant to some things. That thought is short lived however, knowing that *she* is her daughter's advocate. Everything that she has learned along the way has created a clearer path for her on this journey.

Sometimes one parent dives in quickly and spear-heads a lot of the navigation. To me, it seems like many mothers are the lead navigators in the special-needs expedition. Mother's tend to be naturally more nurturing and protective, which appears to fuel our fight. We're often the communicator and wearer of many hats. Not to minimize fathers at all, but mother's are just that — mothers. We get lost in our children. Add autism in the mix and we can become completely submerged. Where do we go from there? We fight, gain access to information, research, pray, and do it all again. Every day! Sometimes we don't think of our impact on other people around us either. Remember when you're engulfed in it, it's hard to reserve energy for anything, or anyone else.

Marriage

Some of the family would get very angry regarding Chelsea's stance on her daughter's needs. This created tension. Sometimes, friends and family would ask Chelsea if she was afraid that her husband would leave her. Her response was that she'd tell him, "peace out!" "I love him to death, and I would die for him, but at the same time, she's my priority," Chelsea said. She feels she has the responsibility to do what's best for her daughter, even at the expense of not appeasing other people's feelings, including her husband. The dynamics of her marriage have somewhat changed. Chelsea is also aware that the divorce rate of parents of children with autism, is extremely high.

Chelsea says that she and her husband talk a lot. They are very open with each other. Coming from a rough childhood, Chelsea says that her husband knows how keeping things bottled up inside, isn't healthy. She also realizes, that he doesn't share everything that he's feeling, all the time. That holds true for lots of men, in general. She never wants him to stuff his emotions down, in a way that will manifest negatively, especially now that he's a family man.

Chelsea explained that they support each other, and are continually getting better at it. They've changed in many ways since Chloe's diagnoses, and are working through the tough parts, together.

Family Matters

When a child is different, out of devastation, parents and other family members often seek a source to blame. The world teaches us all, that in order to effectively fix any problem, you have to find the underlying cause. It's natural for some people, to initially see autism as a problem that needs fixing. Chelsea experienced this first handedly from some relatives.

When Chloe was diagnosed, Chelsea's mom grieved with her. Chelsea's mother-in-law was upset too. She believes that vaccines are one cause of autism among other theories. She also believes that prenatal vitamin consumption, has a part to play in causing autism, according to Chelsea. There was a time Chelsea remembers feeling belittled and offended. It was suggested by a family member that her not taking prenatal vitamins, caused the autism. Little did they know, Chelsea's pregnancy regiment included daily prenatal vitamins.

There are some major differences in the way that Dwayne and Chelsea grew up, and Chelsea sees the results today. Chelsea was raised to work hard and earn things in life. Her husband came form a more privileged upbringing. At the beginning of their life together, they were broke, so it made it easy for his parents to offer financial help, and for the young couple to accept. Over time, Chelsea started to feel uncomfortable with the help. She said it felt a little as if it was held over their heads. Chelsea feels that help should be given free, because someone wants to help. It should be done solely out of the kindness of someone's heart. In this case, for the love of a granddaughter. Despite the differences between Chelsea and her husbands mom, she adores her husband. She expressed how communication is the key which sustains her marriage.

Chelsea doesn't make any big decisions about Chloe without discussing it with her husband first. Being that Dwayne and his mother are close, he sometimes shares with her about these things. This weighs on Chelsea heavily, because she feels it puts her husband in the middle, when his mother doesn't agree with her decisions. It causes tension and friction in their marriage at those times.

Religion and Tradition.

When Chelsea and her husband started dating, they learned pretty quickly that they were raised with different love languages. Her husband enjoyed Chelsea's expression of love and so he's adopted this different appreciation, since they've been together. Chelsea doesn't hold material things in higher value than emotional and spiritual wealth. As a couple, they are trying to teach Chloe to be selfless. They try as best as they can to stay grounded in faith. They also are teaching Chloe some traditions, like putting something on the *Giving Tree,* at their church.Chloe got to pick out an angel from the Giving Tree, and buy a gift for the child it represented. It's not always an angel, but something similar, every year during the holidays. It may take more practice and repetition, but Chelsea and her husband are determined to help Chloe learn traditions that are important to them.

Due to special needs, Chelsea had to adapt her view and modify her approach in education for her daughter. It has been an immense shift and has required a ton of energy. Being that she has spent so much effort on the educational piece, she feels too tapped out to try and do the same regarding religion for Chloe. Chelsea hasn't found a church that is the perfect fit for her daughter. It's not easy for her to default to another religious practice at this point in her life, even if it has more supports for her daughter in place.

Chelsea's husband refers to himself and his wife as, "cafeteria Catholics." He was raised mostly without religion, and she was raised with it, as mentioned. On top of that, she voices the accommodations that are necessary for her daughter to participate in church. Chelsea has seen many special-needs families in similar situations regarding religion. It's true that for us church goers, we're often trying to find one that fits, or to change it to fit. Chelsea shared that being Catholic, she's had a negative experience in exploring attending a Christian non-denominational church. Once they were aware that she practiced Catholicism, she felt like she was judged by some of the congregation. Even still, she wants her daughter to know God in some way; to recognize a creator. Chelsea feels that it's very important to have faith, otherwise you'll be stuck sulking in a life you didn't plan for. I agree with Chelsea on this 100 percent. I also know how hard it is when your church doesn't have a space for your child to belong, or doesn't have accommodations that make it welcoming for them.

In finding a church, Chelsea visited several to get a feel for them before trying to bring her daughter to services. Change is already difficult for Chloe. It would be something new, so Chelsea has to be sure she is comfortable enough to invest in that endeavor. *Applied behavior analysis (ABA)*, a therapy common for helping kids with autism, can help teach kids how to get through tough transitions a little easier. It can definitely help build functional routines, even church routines.

Starting ABA

The struggle for getting good early intervention services started, was real. Prior to receiving the official diagnosis of autism, Chelsea had pinned several things on *Pinterest*, related to speech and autism. A high-school friend of her husband's (who's in the field of ABA) noticed right away. She reached out to Chelsea, asking if they suspected that Chloe had autism. Chelsea explained that they were in the process of getting evaluations done. The friend offered to help if needed. After the diagnosis she offered to attended meetings, and to be available for support as much as she could be. What an amazing human, I have to say! She did end up helping the family bypass a waiting list, when Chloe first started ABA therapy, which was indeed a huge help. This friend helped pave the way to find services at the beginning of the family's autism journey, and they are forever grateful for that.

The Dental Challenge

How would ABA help Chloe exactly? Well, there are several things that this type of therapy can help with. ABA can help children with autism become learning ready, and learn how to accomplish tasks that come easily to typically developing children. Different programs can be developed such as, desensitization programs for hair cutting, or teeth cleaning. These programs help to make those experiences tolerable to some degree, and meaningful. After our brief discussion on ABA, an incident came to mind for Chelsea. She shared about her experience in trying to take Chloe to have dental work done. This was without the support of ABA.

Chelsea had a difficult time with Chloe at the dental office she took her to. Chloe has to be sedated in order to have work done properly. Chelsea was informed that she would not be allowed in the room with her daughter while the procedure was being performed. She didn't feel comfortable having her child sedated, and not being able to be in the room with her. The dentist told Chelsea that she wouldn't do the work, because their "personalities conflicted," Chelsea said. Oh my gosh, I don't even know what I would've done, or said! The dentist wanted Chelsea to agree to treatment in writing, before they actually knew if tooth extraction was necessary. Chelsea would not agree. She has since struggled to find a good fit in a dentist for her daughter. This was only one of the many battles Chelsea has encountered since Chloe's diagnoses. There have been other challenges along the way, including those surrounding public education.

Public Education: The Little Battles

Chelsea was really scared about sending her daughter to public school. At three years old, children with autism are referred to their local school district. Right off the back, Chelsea noticed that the classroom

Chloe was going to be in (an *ALB* classroom) was under staffed. Chelsea complained to the school about it. She told them that she'd have to take it to the school board, if something wasn't done. This was the beginning of the family's public education experience and it didn't start on the right foot.

When it was time for Chloe to start her ALB preschool, the proper student-teacher ratio was in place. It appears that Chelsea was heard. Hold the breaks though, another problem quickly surfaced.

Chloe was an *eloper*. There was a busy parking lot between her classroom and the cafeteria. The kids in the classroom were expected to walk across the parking lot to the cafeteria — I bet you can see where this is going! Chloe was a picky eater and Chelsea didn't want Chloe to have to walk with the other kids across campus due to safety issues. Being a picky eater, she'd bring her own lunch to school, so there was no need to go to the cafeteria. Remember how they had just got the classroom ratio right? Seems like that wasn't going to be the only problem at this school site.

Chelsea asked the lunch lady if there was a way to have the meals delivered to the classroom. The lunch lady couldn't understand the problem; the potential dangers of children that wander. Chelsea had to take it up with the principal when the lunch lady wasn't willing to budge. The teachers and aides, had actually already tried to address the problem with no success.

Chelsea feels like many times the district employees are only there for a paycheck. They sometimes might even use what Chelsea thinks is an excuse, that they have a full caseload. On the other hand she knows that sometimes they do. She knows friends that have left their public education positions, because of that very reason. Chelsea understands this reality, but ultimately feels like it's not a good enough excuse. Chelsea made the point that those professionals are there to do a job and the districts needs to support them to get it done. Here we were simply talking about an issue during non-academic time. What other hiccups, if you will, would little Chloe and Chelsea have to face in school?

Speech at School

Chloe attended the same school for three years, in a pre-k through kinder ALB classroom. The entire time, the speech therapist kept saying that Chloe couldn't use an *augmentative and alternative communication (AAC)* device, and wasn't making progress. Chelsea knew this speech therapist didn't believe in her daughter, but that didn't detour her belief in Chloe one bit. Uh oh, this sounds similar to another story in this book.

The speech therapist wasn't wanting to submit Chelsea's request for use of an AAC device for Chloe. The classroom teacher signed the form, and still, the speech therapist was reluctant to do so. Chelsea took it upon herself to get ahold of the *Assistive Technology (AT)* Specialist. The speech therapist didn't appear to like that. Regardless, per Chloe's AT evaluation, she was granted an AAC device. Way-to-go Chelsea! Sometimes that's how battles are won. I say, when you believe in your child's potential, don't let anything get in the way.

The school started Chloe on an application called, *Talk Tablet*, that Chelsea didn't like. "She was getting it, but it didn't flow for her," Chelsea said. On top of that, no one knew how to use this application! Chelsea felt like they were using the bare minimum, which hindered Chloe from expanding her vocabulary.

Chloe's *triennial* was approaching, the district didn't know yet, but the family would be moving. They were looking for a new house in another school district. Chelsea knew that the device and application needed to change. It turned out that the reason they gave Chloe the device and application they did, is because there wasn't any other available. Chelsea was infuriated! She knew it was within her daughter's legal right, to be provided with an application that is best suited for her to learn with. Chelsea demanded a specific application suitable for her daughter, along with an iPad before the end of that school year. The new application that Chloe started using was called, *LAMB*. Chelsea worked tirelessly with her daughter to help her build skills on the device.

From the time Chloe was a baby, Chelsea presented educational technology apps and material to her. Chelsea feels that it served the benefit of making learning with an AAC device much easier for Chloe. At three years old, Chloe only had very few words. Now at around five years old, she was learning to use an AAC device to communicate. By the end of that school year, Chloe amazed everyone with what she was able to do.

In the last year alone, Chloe jumped to well over twenty-five words that she was saying. "She sings all the time," Chelsea said. Chelsea attributes this success in part, due to moving her daughter from one school district to another. Also the appropriate AAC device and application made a world of difference. The new school district is one that Chelsea felt had better supports in place for her daughter.

Like many parents of limited or emerging communicators, Chelsea interchanges the words, "nonverbal" and "preverbal", to describe her daughter's language abilities. With Chloe's immense growth in language, she may even be looking at dropping both of these terms all together. Surely something the previous school speech therapist never imagined.

After attending the three-year long ALB classroom at the first school, the family moved to a new school district. For first grade, Chloe started attending a *special day classroom(SDC)*.[5] Most of the other students in her class appeared to have autism as well.

At the school Chloe attended before switching districts, the speech therapist did not seem to understand what she needed. Chelsea says that her daughter needs to find things personally meaningful, in order to be engaged. Then, once you've found that, you can slip things in that are not highly preferred. At the new school she attends, Chelsea refers to the speech therapist as, "the Chloe Whisperer." This particular therapist caught

---

[5] Special Day Classroom (SDC), is where students with varying disabilities are placed, either in mild to moderate, or moderate to severe classrooms.

on to what makes Chloe tick. Now, Chloe is talking more than every before! Chelsea says she dreamed of her daughter being able to talk. She dreamed and prayed that she would *hear* her talk. "When it starts to happen, you're not prepared," Chelsea said. She is still somewhat in disbelief that her daughter's verbal language is actually emerging. I can only imagine what that's like. Chelsea described what she felt upon hearing Chloe start to talk as, "you know in high school where the boy likes you…it's the same thing, different circumstance, it's crazy," she said. "You're happy, you're giddy, you're excited, same feeling, totally different circumstance," Chelsea added.

The Price to Speak

Chloe continued to receive both speech therapy privately and at school. ABA was started, and the family was paying out of pocket for private speech therapy from a company that worked well with autism. Chelsea says that there was just NO WAY, to pay for additional speech services! More speech is always beneficial, but their insurance plan didn't cover services from this particular provider. Switching to another plan under the same insurance company could remedy that, but leave Chloe without other services that were covered under her current plan. If they could do more they would. Chloe was thriving in speech therapy.

We know she started taking off with talking, but how did the process of attending speech look for Chloe? As it turns out, it was much like many of our experiences. Chelsea described her drop-off experience, which you might relate to. She says that Chloe can go into therapy looking ready to go and happy to be there. Some days however, as soon as the door closes, Chelsea can hear her child screaming! We agree, that as parents of children going to different therapies, we learn to grow tough skin, figuratively speaking. You have to learn to walk away and not always try to rescue at the first sign of protest from your child. Then when you start to see results, you know that your tough love paid off. I think this is something that many parents of children with autism struggle with. It's almost like fighting against your instinct to protect your child, but you know it's for the best. It might take some of us as much practice at adapting, as it does our children. Nonetheless, speech has remained consistent for Chloe, even when new issues arise in different environments.

New Placement New Issues

Chelsea didn't run into the same problems at Chloe's new school, as she did at the previous one. However, some issues came up that created a rocky start at this new school.

When we take on any new endeavor, we can find ourselves holding our breath, waiting for the other shoe to drop. Almost as if the new placement was too good to be true for Chelsea, new issues surfaced.

First, There was one incident that was a result of a misunderstanding regarding an email. One day, when Chelsea arrived at the school with Chloe, the teacher had a rather worried look on her face.

She was a young non-credentialed teacher, "not yet jaded," according to Chelsea. Chelsea went through the routine of drop-off with Chloe. This included things like, placing her backpack in a basket, finding her morning schedule, etc. On her way out, Chelsea asked the teacher if anything was wrong, because of the worried look she had. Chelsea shared that she doesn't do well with sad emotions. The teacher asked if she could speak to her outside. Then, the teacher broke out into tears and apologized to Chelsea. Wait, what?

Chelsea still wasn't sure what this was all about, but then the teacher mentioned an email that Chelsea had sent. It just so happened that Chelsea wasn't sure if her daughter's classroom was going to participate in the school's Christmas performance that year. She had sent an email to the teacher to inquire about it. Being that the district they were in before rarely included the children with special needs like this, she was simply asking a question. She didn't mean anything else by the email. She honestly wasn't sure if she had missed something that got sent home about the Christmas performance, because she hadn't heard anything. "I literally thought I missed it, and this woman was crying," Chelsea said. Chelsea was pretty nervous and kept wondering if she had slipped some not-so polite jargon into that email. She had a drink with her dinner that night she sent the email, whoopsie! It turned out that the teacher felt really bad, because she actually didn't have the news letter ready with the information on the Christmas program in a timely manner, hence the crying. Apparently after that point, Chelsea became the class mom.

To help the teacher feel better (and make light of the situation) Chelsea suggested they do something in the classroom. She shared over the phone what had transpired in the classroom to her husband. He couldn't help but laugh. Chloe's classroom had their very own mini-performance for Christmas. All was well in the world, at least in the classroom.

There are both pros and cons to the new school placement in Chelsea's opinion. One of the pros is that there are opportunities that are available for her daughter. Chelsea looks forward to the fourth-grade through sixth-grade classroom placement for Chloe. She feels that the first-grade through third-grade teacher lacks in experience, and it can impede on opportunities.

Another issue took place during Chloe's first week of school at this placement. She got hurt. Chelsea was disappointed that she was not made aware that her daughter's classroom participated in mainstream recess. She was also a bit upset that no one could tell her what exactly happened to her daughter. On that particular day, the regular teacher was away doing a mandatory training that the district requires their teachers. Chelsea and her husband were very upset that their petite child, didn't have the attention she required. They did receive a phone call, were told that everything was fine, and that Chloe had a small red mark above her eye. Chelsea asked that they call her if anything changed. When Chloe got home the small bump had swollen to the size of a golf ball, and bruised! For this reason, Chelsea called an emergency *IEP*.

During that IEP another injury was discussed. Chloe's parents concluded that Chloe's aide wasn't being as diligent as needed. It was also determined that the team needed to create more visual supports for Chloe. Sometimes parents feel like they are bringing more to the table than the "professionals" sitting across from them. As a parent, that's not the best feeling. Chelsea and her husband didn't like that they had to point out obvious things that should have been taken care of by the school.

Chelsea has had to weigh the options of seeking legal action versus compromising with the school districts, often. They've found more positive aspects compared to the prior school placement, making it easier to compromise here. Chelsea feels that sometimes being the squeaky wheel breaks the relationships, including the positive ones that Chloe has made. Chelsea wasn't sure she'd want to risk losing the incredible relationship, her daughter and the speech therapist had established. She believes she has to pick and choose her battles wisely.

Chloe is currently learning to make friends, some of which are *neurotypical*. She is learning social appropriateness. Chelsea tries not to step in to stop things she knows Chloe won't like, for instance receiving hugs. However, she makes sure to use those as teachable moments directly for her daughter, and indirectly for others. On a positive note, Chelsea sees her daughter's school as the perfect place to get that social piece. Let's face it, the right educational program can be rather difficult to find for a child with autism.

If a Cure Existed

With educational battles in mind, among other challenges, if Chelsea could rid her daughter of autism and all her conditions, part of her would want to. She would say "yes" to a cure, due the struggles. Life is hard, speaking is hard, as well as making friends for Chloe. Those are the things Chelsea would love to see made easier for her daughter. However, she's happy in her

196

world, and Chelsea says, "I wouldn't know Chloe any other way." It's a hard and conflicting decision for her to ponder. On the other hand, Chelsea is confident that her husband would choose to rid their daughter of her conditions, if it was an option — no questions asked.

Being an only child, her husband hasn't been around many children, Chelsea says. She feels like when there's any problem, he just wants it fixed right away, like many fathers do. Also, being in the military, he was trained to put his emotions aside. In the ten years they've been together, she's only seen him cry twice. She thinks that's all part of why he'd choose to cure Chloe's autism. It's a HUGE thing for dads to accept the disability, but that does NOT mean they love their children any less.

Suggestions for Others

Chelsea believes that everyone should give themselves some time in their journey with autism, to deal with the emotional impact it brings. If you don't, she warns that it can sneak up on you when you least expect it. You can get stuck searching for answers, and lose yourself there.

Chelsea feels that many parents are quick to dismiss their instincts. She thinks it's not in the best interest of their children. She suggests to rise up to the challenge, and that there's a way to do that without being confrontational.

On the other hand, she encourages educators, should they suspect something is wrong or not working for a student, to do something about it. Overall, Parents need to be brave enough to do what's best for their child. It could be homeschooling for some, and it could be public eduction for others. She also feels that parents should be willing to sacrifice a whole lot, to do what's best for their child. Chelsea says, "Follow your gut, and ask tons of questions!"

My Take

In Chelsea's story, there is a theme that stood out to me. She described how a marriage works with autism in the mix. Not every marriage is the same obviously, but the success of it depends on some important things that apply to all relationships. Communication, support and love. Chelsea describes the difficulty of accepting her daughter's diagnoses and how her husband was there for her. There were plenty of times that there was friction with extended family, but Chelsea stayed focused on what her daughter needed. Even though her husband wasn't as ambitious as Chelsea about the assessments and therapies initially, she still went through with things and he ultimately supported her decisions. To me, that signifies a very strong relationship worth mentioning.

I can appreciate their dynamic. It makes me realize that not everything will be pleasant in marriages all the time, even for the best ones. Autism can definitely complicate things, and everyone has the right to their own feelings regarding the difficulties. Statistics are not in favor of married parents of children with autism. The divorce rate is pretty high, and you can imagine all the reasons why!

When Chelsea explained that her husband is a veteran, and mentioned how he buries his emotions sometimes, it sounds all too familiar to me. Not the veteran part, but the emotional part. My kids' father, my friend's husbands, and so on and so forth, have a hard time talking about the hard parts of autism, a lot of the time. I believe support for fathers is a huge need in our community. With FAN, I started the Autism Dad's Support Group, so the guys can get together, doing "guy things". From what I hear, the few times they've gotten together, it has been great! They do end up talking about their kids with autism. I really wasn't sure how that would unfold. As moms, there's a lot out there for us, but not so much for the dads. At least not a lot that they're willing to be involved in, it seems.

Chelsea also described some of the fight that she's had to go through with her young daughter in school, which is an unfortunate reality. The situations she mentioned left me wanting to offer suggestions for remedying anything I knew how to. That took me back to many battles I've had to face with my son's education. It made me remember how often, and how hard we have to fight for the rights of our children with autism.

CHAPTER 7

"He Birthed My Soul"

This is the story of Stacee's journey with autism.
This one's filled with heart aching experiences and monumental hope. Stacee's son suffers form *MTHFR gene mutations.* It took many twists and turns, for Stacee to learn of her son's condition. You'll often hear about young children with autism. Thus far in this book, you have read about the mother's experiences of children ranging from toddlers to teens. Adam, Stacee's son, is a young adult living with a form of autism.

Sitting on my glider, feet kicked up on my ottoman and laptop in hand, I listened to Stacee's story over the phone. This was one of the only interviews that did not take place in person, yet her voice conveyed all the emotion entailed in her story. Stacee was thoroughly descriptive. She painted her journey with special needs in such a unique way. Her son being a young adult, shed a different light for me, and surely will for many of you who read it.

Introducing Adam

Stacee had children with her ex-husband, of which Adam was the second oldest. She described Adam as a chubby faced infant, as a baby. Her son seemed to be developing perfectly and thriving. At ten months old, she taught him how to sign the word, "more." Then, a few months later, she remembers starting to see changes in her son. With every vaccine she clearly remembers something physically going on with him. "Clearly something was happening," Stacee says. He would bang his head and he was very unsteady on his feet it seemed. By thirteen months old, Adam was no longer engaging in play, and he never started talking.

In the years that followed, Stacee was relentless to get to the bottom of what had happened to her son. She had him undergo a series of blood work and tests. Through these tests, it was found that *mercury and thimerosal* were two chemicals detected at elevated levels in Adam's system. In past years, those chemicals were used in vaccines. Stacee mentioned that thimerosal wasn't removed from some vaccines until until after 1996. In fact, according to an article by the Illinois Department of Public Health, thimerosal was finally removed from all childhood vaccines with the exception of multi-dose influenza vaccines, in 2001 (2020). Her son received vaccines containing this chemical prior to that date. She worked with a geneticist, who determined that Adam couldn't expel the toxins from thimerosal, and his body couldn't tolerate it.

Up Against A Wall

Still, Stacee sought out more answers. She knew she needed to get help for her son in some way and quickly. Why was her son sick all the time? What did his behaviors mean? Why wasn't he talking yet? Doctors often left her with no real answers. She then went to an *integrative medical clinic*. It was there that Adam was found to have an overgrowth of yeast in his blood. This is a condition known as *candida*. At the time, it was very difficult for Stacee to make sense of everything. She says, "There were lots of things looking back that popped up." However, at that time she felt like she was up against a wall, drowning — a feeling many special-needs parents can relate to. While searching to understand her son's behaviors completely, and get him the help he needed, Stacee's world was spinning out of control around her.

Sinking Ship

Stacee wasn't finding much support in her search efforts. Adam's father had his head in the sand, figuratively speaking. Then when Adam was six years old, he was finally assessed at the *University of California, San Francisco (UCSF)*. Adam was diagnosed with *autism spectrum disorder (ASD)*. They could put a name on it, something that explained his behaviors. This meant that services could begin. Although, it did not predict the quality of services which would transpire. During the preschool years Adam was self-injurious. Stacee shared, "it was a living nightmare." As if that wasn't enough for her to deal with, her marriage was falling apart. It ultimately ended in divorce. In 2004, Adam's father relinquished all rights to his son. According to Stacie, "he felt he wasn't cut out for this." Stacy was now a single mother, headed to embark on the journey of special needs.

The Journey Begins

The fight for services was over the top. Stacee felt like she had defeated one giant in getting her son diagnosed. Her neighbor had given her a book called, "Let me Hear Your Voice". This book introduced Stacee to *ABA* therapy, and offered her hope in future possibilities fo her son, with the right supports in place. She then found herself fighting to get things in order for her son with special-education, and the regional center. That wasn't going well. Stacee's eyes were opened to what her son needed, and still, she was being made to feel as if he wasn't *capable* of learning.

Stacie knew that Adam needed supports in place at school, but that wasn't happening.

He couldn't even sit in a chair. "He was suffering in the classroom," Stacee said. From three to five years old, Adam's preschool services were lousy. Stacee had to inform the school that she would go to the *Special Education Local Plan Area (SELPA)*, if changes weren't made.

Once the school was aware that Stacee knew her rights, the program she was fighting for was finally given to her son. Adam had two years of skill based success in school. He learned how to tie his own shoes. He also learned to write his own name. At seven years old, Adam had a year of mainstreaming, in which he did amazingly! Stacee was thrilled to see the difference in her son, all due to having the right supports in place for him. Life seemed to be taking a turn in the right direction.

Obstacles and Hurdles

It wasn't long before Stacee was once again devastated. Her son received the short end of the stick yet again, after overcoming poor early intervention.

After the school year of mainstream ended, she was ready for Adam to reflect the same progress through summer. Sadly, the program that was in place for him couldn't remain staffed. All momentum was lost, and it was completely detrimental for Adam. Though it was tough, Stacee didn't stop fighting for her son. She filed *due process,* and she won.

There was enough documentation to prove that there were clear violations of the *Individuals with Disabilities Education Act (IDEA)* surrounding Adam's education. He was then placed in an ABA day-school in Santa Cruz, California. It was a year-round school. It provided continuity and allowed for Stacee to work. Then after Adam was twelve years old, the placement was no longer a good fit for him. This was another crossroads for Stacee.

Adam was going through bio-chemical changes, due to a medication he was taking. Adam's behavior had become increasingly difficult to manage at home. When Adam was almost fifteen years old, he was hospitalized.

"He needed to be stabilized," Stacee said. Adam had to be restrained two different times in the hospital during his stay. Stacee hated that this had to be done. He was extremely medicated. This was difficult for Stacee, but she knew he needed to get stable before they could move forward. It was unbearable for her to watch her son go through it all. She said, "he went to the door and didn't want to stay, like a little child not wanting to stay at a church daycare." Stacee just wanted her baby well. She never wanted this for him!

The day after Adam was admitted into the hospital, all services were lost. Stacee was distressed and had let everything go, in dealing with the events that lead up to the hospitalization. She lost her job and *In Home Supportive Services* (*IHSS*) was gone. She let the rent go and got evicted. She was living in a high cost area, and didn't want to be living off of welfare, but everything was gone. This was a very scary, and dark time in her life. Luckily she had the support of her parents, her brother, and a friend. Her friend is an advocate for her own son, and has been by Stacee's side since Adam was about three years old. Stacee realizes how blessed she was to have the support she had, and she never forgets it. Also unforgettable to Stacee was a very special person she met during that time.

You may be familiar with the notion that mother's lose themselves in their children, and I've referenced that quite a few times in these stories already. Sometimes we need to remember who we are as individuals. As you can imagine, Stacee lost herself in motherhood and special needs. One evening while making her usual rounds from the hospital to home, Stacee decided to stop at a venue her father was performing at. Her father is a musician. Stacee recalls, "It was June 3rd, 2010." She didn't have to go home right away, and she met a nice young man who she danced with. She felt like a "woman of her age" for the first time, in what seemed like forever! Little did she know, the turn her life was about to take.

Stacee and the gentleman she met that night started dating. He would travel every weekend to see her and help with her kids. She never thought that she'd find someone who would step into that role. She had made peace with being a single mother, being engulfed in special needs already. Her new boyfriend was extremely supportive.

By September of 2010, Adam got full wraparound care through regional center. He spent a total of five months every day, with full *IHSS* hours as well. Ironically, years before, when Stacee first sought out IHSS services, Adam was denied. During a home visit, a psychologist gave Adam a high five, and proceeded to determine at that time, that Adam didn't qualify for *respite*.[6] Lesson here, if denied, apply again. A few years can make a huge difference for some services that are funded through agencies like CVRC.

---

[6]Respite-this type of care for special-needs persons is used by many autism families, providing care for the special-needs child, for a limited amount of time. Respite is sometimes funded and available to families at no cost.

In the spring of 2011, Stacee enrolled in school to pursue a post-secondary nutritional holistic coaching degree. During that same year, she and her boyfriend got married and became a blended family. It was one of the happiest times in Stacee's life. The family moved to Visalia, California. She learned that services were fully integrated there, which meant she wouldn't have to fight for services the same way anymore. She adds, "I had a prestine IEP." Stacee could breathe a little easier now.

Prior to Adam's hospitalization the year before, Stacee had worked for a company that helped with brain detoxification and nutrition. In 2013, at her new place of work, while creating a dietary plan for a client, the blood work looked strikingly familiar to Stacee. She knew she had seen something nearly identical before. Stacee couldn't shake the notion, and pulled up her own son's blood work. It was uncanny that it nearly identically mirrored Adam's blood work, leading to a very important discovery. The two sets of blood work showed the same MTHFR gene mutation.

Everything came rushing back to Stacie like scenes from a movie, when the answer was there all along. She wondered how she missed that in her line of work. Was her field of expertise a mere coincidence? She felt immense guilt. As she learned more, she was flooded with more guilt! "It was like being in an alternate universe," Stacee said.

When her ex-husband abandoned her, she had no other options. She did only what she knew how to do for her son. She thought she was fighting the right fight, and now felt like she left a huge piece of her son's puzzle (no pun intended), dismissed. She remembered how people told her to put him in a home, when Adam was seven years old, because of his destructive behavior. She remembered feeling as if she was in a prison without the walls. She couldn't put anything like pictures or home decor up on the actual walls, because he would take them off and tear them apart. As far as outings, she couldn't do the normal things. She couldn't take her children to the movies! Adam was little, so it just looked

213

like misbehavior to the passerby, but it was more than that.

The flood of memories of fighting with the school, rejection by his own father, from his family, and societal rejections, all came rushing back to Stacee. She would constantly try to cut corners and lower the bar in a sense, for her family's well being. It was a hard life for Adam — for the entire family.

Stacy feels like she was deprived of her son, out of fear. "He was sidelined out of life by vaccine injury," she said. She feels that because she didn't know any better, her son was robbed of his potential, by her allowing him to receive vaccines. She was afraid of what would happen if she didn't let him get those immunizations done.

On the flip side, Stacee also feels that the hard work has afforded her a beautiful life now. It's still emotionally and physically painful, that her son can't express his hopes and dreams to her. I can completely empathize with Stacee there. It is a pain that no one can understand unless it's part of their life.

She worries that Adam can't tell her if anyone is hurting him. It's a constant reminder of her guilt. On top of everything, Stacee sometimes wonders what life would have been like, if Adam's father would've been more involved.

Family Impact

Life with special needs has been hard on all of Adams siblings. Stacee's children from her first marriage, wanted to play with their brother, but frustration was inevitable. They loved him, but at times hated how he behaved with them when they were young. "Ruling life by the liability was difficult," Stacee said. Their world was literally turned upside down to accommodate special needs. When Adam turned eighteen years old, things got tough again. Stacee and her new husband had their first baby together. With a new baby and an adult child that needed help getting dressed, it wasn't easy, to say the least.

During a visit at the behavioral health clinic, the doctor found that the dose of medication Adam was prescribed to manage his behavior, was higher than necessary. Time was of the essence and Stacee didn't want to lose any more precious time for her son. They quickly remedied his medication regiment. Stacee did what she could to help resolve any behavioral issues, and made sure to leave no stone unturned.

Adult Placement

Adam wasn't happy at home anymore. Stacee and the rest of the family were exhausted. "It was time," Stacee said. He needed a change. Adam went into placement a little over five years ago. He was in a living facility, *level IV group home*, which included behavioral support. The initial arrangement however, was problematic. Poor Stacee! It seems as though she constantly ran into setbacks, at every new turn.

When Adam first went into placement, Stacee was undergoing a legal matter. Like many things she had to learn along the way, assuming guardianship of her son, was another one to add to the list. Once a CVRC client reaches the age of majority, if someone isn't stipulated to assume guardianship, the agency does. This is what happened in Adam's case. It was a long drawn out process, that left Stacee with very little control over decisions, regarding placement for her son, until it was resolved.

In Adam's first placement, the manager told Stacee, "he's ours." Stacee also witnessed mistreatment of other clients. She had special, size twelve shoes made for Adam at a store called, the *Boot Emporium*. When he was sent home for a weekend, Adam's new shoes were missing, and he was in a pair two sizes too small. Stacee felt this environment was harmful to her son. As soon as she possibly could, she got him out of there.

Stacee found a better placement for Adam. He started thriving again. Yay! He became a star student and was doing great. One setback happened when his teacher left without any notice. At that time, Adam started a *perseveration* behavior, of drinking water. This led to a condition knowns as *hyponatremia,* which he almost died from. He was hospitalized, and by God's grace made a full recovery. It must have been incredibly frightening! It was a miracle that he survived.

Adam eventually graduated from the *Adult Transition Program (ATP).* Stacee said, "I balled like a baby." This was a monumental moment for the family. Stacee felt that after all her fight, and her son's struggle, he beat the odds in so many ways. Adam was then moved to another placement for ages nineteen to twenty-one years old. Both Stacee and Adam formed a strong bond with one of the workers there. They learned he would be opening up his own special-needs living program. Stacee was looking forward to eventually moving her son there.

Stacee's View of Autism

When pregnant with one of Adam's younger siblings, Stacee learned that she herself was also an MTHFR gene mutation carrier. She experienced a condition called *Hashimotos.* As it would turn out, Adam didn't only have one gene mutation, he had two, making it nearly impossible to *methylate*. This meant it was difficult for his body to build and breakdown proteins, as well as other chemicals. This mutation can cause Autistic-like symptoms to surface in some people.

For Stacee, it's not really autism that she see's in her son. She see's Adam as vaccine injured, with Autistic-like symptoms. She Also sees autism as a way for certain forces to shine light away form issues with vaccines. One good thing, according to Stacee, is that autism was a means to get services for her son. She adds, "it's a blessing and a curse." If there were a way to rid her son of his conditions, legal, safe, all upside, no down side, she would be all for that.

Finding Her Heroes

Stacee shared that she loves her son Adam, and that she believes an infinite God loves him more. "My faith has played a pre-imminent role in my survival and hope," Stacee said. Her faith has kept her grounded through the struggle and pain. She also feels that Adam's struggles have made her more *human*. This journey has made her grow up; made her find the hero inside, clarify relationships, and learn the capacity of her own strength and faith.

As a child, Stacee had learning difficulties that affected her life. When she looks back now, she thinks that God was preparing her for what was yet to come. As an adult, she also remembers thinking that if she had children that weren't "normal" or healthy, she'd accept them just the way they are. She had a sense of maternal, unconditional love, before Adam was even born. Stacee taught her other children that Adam's life has value, and that is something that should never be thrown away! She says that her adult children have become people with huge hearts and compassion.

Stacy says that in his life, Adam has taken her soul and heart, and expanded them outward. Her son is *her* hero. She has never seen anyone more brave or strong. Stacee is certain that given the right supports, Adam will always surpass anything put in front of him.

"It's just my job to set the stage," she adds. Stacee says, "I gave birth to him physically, but he birthed my soul." I seriously needed tissues when she said that powerful statement — wow!

Learning Through Her Journey

In her journey with special needs, Stacee teaches other parents several things. Trust your instincts! Ask for genetic testing. You can rule out physical and genetic conditions with simple blood work. Also, never lose hope in your child's potential. Maintain your faith, and fight fiercely for what they need.

My Take

This is one story that is emotionally evoking for me. Stacee really went through a whole lot in her journey with autism. The sibling impact is touched on here again. Her son was vaccine injured, and she was filled with an abundance of guilt in learning this reality. Her talk about guilt, strikes a nerve with me. It makes me acknowledge all the things I've felt guilty of, in my own journey as a mother of special-needs children. It's a guilt brought about, when learning that small things done differently, could have made a big difference. Hearing about Stacee's guilt actually made me feel okay with my own.

Stacee shared about her son's struggles from rejection, to medication, and acquiring the supports he deserved in life. Thinking about similar elements in my son's life, had me reaching for tissues. Her experience of his struggles, my heart knows some of those feelings very well.

Stacee's son does have MTHFR gene mutations, so her story brings the varying dynamics within the autism community, to surface. It is interesting to me how she doesn't really see her son as having autism, but rather being vaccine injured. In my situation with my son, genetic testing has not revealed any causal cues. In a sense, having the "cause" answer, is something that many parents including myself, want at some point in their journey with special needs. Stacee was afforded that knowledge, which she only wishes she knew sooner.

Another thing I learned through this story, was about the importance of obtaining guardianship when our children reach the age of majority. It scares me to think how easily in the whirlwind of life, something so simple can be missed. I made sure to meet with my son's social worker and discuss this, after hearing about Stacees long battle to resume guardianship of her son. I'm also aware that there are some incidences, where allowing an agency to assume that responsibility, might be in the best interest of the client.

Finally, the reality that special-needs children grow up, was displayed through this story. Things that may be easy to dismiss when a child is younger, might be more difficult to manage easily, later on. Stacee's story reminds me of the importance of good quality early intervention. It also makes me remember that life goes on beyond special needs.

Stacie is a mother led by faith, and believes that God has a purpose for her son. She eloquently describes how her son played a part in making her soul come alive, and how God loves him more than she ever can. Her perspective made quite an impression on me.

CHAPTER 8

Ultimately Autism

A few years back I had the opportunity to meet another amazing mother. Her name is Paula. Throughout the years, Paula and her son have attended events hosted by Fresno Autism Network (FAN).

I ran into Paula again while at a mariachi performance with the group I used to play with. In case I didn't mention it, I play the violin. As it turns out, at this function I learned that one of Paula's cousins worked at my doctor's office. I met her when I was going to my appointments prior to having my first baby; my son who ended up having autism.

Paula's son is a few years older than mine, and she was already raising a differently abled child before my son was born. I think it's interesting how different paths in life cross sometimes. More recently, Paula has assisted FAN in helping with events, and providing venue space at her place of work.

Life As She Knew It

Paula lives with her parents in Fresno, California. She has one child named Patrick, or Pat for short.Patrick has *autism spectrum disorder (ASD)*. A little over sixteen years ago, Paula's life changed in a big way. She was an independent working woman, killing it at her job. She had no distractions in her life. Paula was enjoying her time hanging out with good friends and family. She was looking forward to getting a promotion at work, and she was well on on her way. She was a woman content with her life.

Paula came from a large Hispanic family. When she wasn't busy at work, she spent a great deal of time at various family functions. She thought her life would remain the same..forever. Life definitely had other plans for Paula. New doors began opening, including one she didn't plan for.

Paula became pretty stressed at work, feeling tired and overwhelmed. She thought it was a good idea to take a some time off. Paula realized that she *really* wasn't feeling very well, even after taking the time off. She ended up making herself a doctor's appointment to get to the bottom of how she was feeling. The doctor ran a series of tests on her. The results revealed something completely life changing. Paula was shocked to learn the she was—pregnant!

The news came at the same time some other major changes in Paula's life were happening. She had just received that promotion at work and she was newly single. Paula had so many questions. What would this mean regarding her promotion? How was she supposed to be a single mother? After the initial panic dissolved, she figured she was as ready as she'd ever be. She also had the support of her family. That was a HUGE blessing.

Expectations

Paula didn't know she was pregnant. It was a total surprise. She starting reflecting on the prior few months. Did she consume alcohol in the first months before she knew? Did she unknowingly do anything that could have caused harm to her growing baby? She knew she didn't take prenatal vitamins until her second trimester. She was concerned about her baby's health. The mama bear was already there, wanting to protect her baby, even from her own mistakes. I'd say this was a great mom in the making. Wouldn't you agree?

Paula had continued working up until a week before her actual due date. When she went into the hospital to have the baby, things didn't go according to plan. Having high blood pressure played a role in the decision for doctors to perform a *cesarian section*. Patrick was born that Friday at 8:07am. The family happily welcomed the new little bundle home. He was a healthy happy baby.

Grandmas know Best

Paula explained that her mom (Grandma), runs an in-home daycare, which she had been doing for eighteen years already. When Pat was around nine months old, he started attending the daycare. There were a few other babies around the same age there as well. Grandma noticed that Pat wasn't reaching certain milestones at the same time as the other babies. It had been a couple years, and she was still noticing differences between her grandson's development, and the other kids' in the daycare. Whenever she'd notice something, she'd bring up her concerns to her daughter.

When Patrick was two years old, another child the same age became potty trained, but Pat wasn't. The other kids were getting ready for preschool. It seemed like Patrick wasn't quite ready for that transition either. These differences were becoming more and more apparent. Paula figured it had to be because Pat was just comfortable at home with Grandma. It was easy to assume he'd think, for example, "he didn't have to ask for the cereal like the other kids, because Grandma would do it for him," Paula said. Not asking for things was one thing, but Paula's mother noticed other things too. She would take the other kids outside and "Pat would prefer to hang out inside, in his room, in his own little space, playing his videos," Paula said. Paula was concerned. She had questions. What was going on with her son? Was this just normal kid stuff? Why wasn't he reaching milestones like his peers?

The fire of Paula's search for answers, was further fueled when a nurse came to the daycare. The parents of one little girl at the daycare, had a public health nurse go out to assess their daughter. They had concerns that she had developmental delays. Paula explained that her mom, like some grandmas would, decided to pick that nurses brain and asked questions about her grandson's behavior. The nurse wasn't there for him, but she did notice that Pat seemed to be speech delayed. She suggested that the family reach out to the *Central Valley Regional Center (CVRC)* and schedule an assessment, to rule out any type of developmental delay or condition.

Doctor's Orders

Pat was now three years old, and even after the nurse's suggestion, his doctor insisted that he was fine. Not to mention, the doctor stressed to Paula that Pat was in the 100th percentile for everything physical. Patrick had been seen by that same pediatrician since birth. The doctor told Paula that boys develop slower than girls. He tried to assure Paula that Pat would catch up to his peers in time. Paula knew that something *was* different about her son, but she couldn't put her finger on it. Her mom encouraged her to follow the nurse's advice, but Paula was uncertain now.

Pat had turned three years old that June, and in July they got in for an appointment with CVRC. He was assessed, and they officially determined that Pat was speech delayed. It was then recommended to get him started in an early preschool program called, *Head Start*. This would give him two years to work on the delay, and hopefully be ready for kindergarten. Because he was already three years old, he missed the early intervention window for speech.

School

Patrick attended two years of preschool. During that time, a speech therapist worked with him. He enjoyed going to school. His vocabulary increased, and he was now "potty trained". Woohoo! Paula and her parents saw this all as a HUGE win. After completing the Head Start program, it was time for Patrick to graduate to kindergarten. He was placed in a general education kindergarten classroom, with his prior *individualized education program (IEP)* as a plan to follow.

Everything seemed great. That was, until the teacher informed Paula of Patrick's "outbursts". He started biting! Patrick had never done this before. The teacher suggested that Pat have more assessments done. Paula remembers her mom being hesitant to suggest it, but agreed with the teacher.

The school stressed to Paula that the biting needed to stop! She was spinning her wheels, trying to figure out how to help her son stop biting. Since both the teacher and her mother thought the assessments could be helpful to better understand what was going on with Patrick, Paula seriously started to consider having them done.

Paula has a cousin that worked with special-needs students. Around the time the biting started, Paula reached out to this cousin to get some advice. There was one specific thing that stayed with Paula from her conversations with her cousin. She was advised to never let medication be pushed on Patrick; unless absolutely necessary, but not for his behavior that could be worked on. She also reminded Paula that she could always get a second opinion.

Sounds A Lot Like Pat

During that year, Pat's grandma had to attend a mandatory training for her work, which Paula attended with her. The training would focus on aspects of child development relevant to Grandma's daycare. As far as Pat's development, Paula's mom had a hunch that something still wasn't quite right with her grandson. She believed there was something else going on with him, other than simply a speech delay. Paula says, "she didn't want to be the one to say anything." Nonetheless, she still had her suspicions.

The topic discussed in the training was autism. It covered the general signs and symptoms to look for. When they mentioned things that were very similar to what Paula was seeing in her own son, every whistle went off for her! Some of the symptoms mentioned were things that Patrick exhibited, included things like; the child may be speech delayed, may mimic words, might have outbursts, etc.

Aside from that, Paula realized that her son had *regressed* a little bit in kindergarten. He was having difficulty communicating again, despite the progress he had made over the prior two years. The difficulties with communication were suspected to play a big role in his biting behavior.

When he was in first or second grade, Paula remembers researching and still trying to uncover what was going on with her son. She was convinced that Pat had *Asperger Syndrome*. Part of Paula didn't want to give into the notion of "autism". She explained that she maybe just didn't want her mom to be right. Paula said hearing an, "I told you so," was what she was trying to avoid.

The Autism Assessment in School

In first grade there were some learning challenges, but Paula didn't think too much of it, because it was…only first grade. Paula checked in with the pediatrician, and once again, he didn't see any reason to be concerned with Pat's development or behavior.

Pat would talk at home. School was a different story. He would only say about half the amount of words that he should be saying, from what the speech therapist told Paula. Paula started wondering if maybe Pat had a hearing problem. As you may have guessed, she scheduled an appointment for him to have his hearing checked. The results confirmed that everything was fine with Pat's hearing.

During an IEP when Pat was in the third grade, the speech therapist asked Paula if Pat had ever been assessed for autism. This question stopped Paula in her tracks. She had skirted around the idea of autism for quite a while. She hesitantly agreed to have an autism assessment done by the school. She received the mountainous package of paperwork shortly after the IEP.

I don't know about you, but this took me back! In my own journey with autism, I have found myself dreading all the questionnaires. I did however, develop a rather unique signature, ha! I'm sure Paula has too.

Pat met the criteria to qualify for autism services in the school. Paula didn't know what that entailed, and was still trying to make sense of it all. She had to face the dreaded, "I told you so" from her mother, that she was trying to avoid as mentioned earlier. Oh the ridicule!

In Paula's defense, the concerns were dismissed for so long, she believed it couldn't be autism after all. She also trusted Pat's pediatrician, and the doctor had assured her that Pat was fine — all this time. From then on, Pat's education would be shaped around his autism label.

It's Time to Go Home Pat

In the fourth grade, either Paula's dad (Grandpa) or Paula, would drop off and pick up Pat, at the after-school program at his school. On a rare occasion, Grandpa would walk home from school with Pat. Nothing bad about that, right? A very common thing indeed. However, that played a big role in what transpired next.

One day Paula's mom was outside with the daycare kids. They were playing in her front yard. She happened to glance down the street, to a nearby crosswalk. She saw something that made her do a double take. In the distance, she saw a kid that looked like her grandson, Paula explained. His body, his stature, it looked just like Patrick! Paula's mom told her that the boy was at the intersection, ready to cross it. She tried to disregard thinking it was Patrick, knowing that there was no way he'd be crossing a busy street, or walking home alone for that matter. Besides, it wasn't time for him to be picked up from after-school program.

She couldn't help staring and was worried now that it *was* Patrick. Paula explained that her mother was suddenly flooded with panic! Here she had all these kids playing in her yard, and the one kid, she suspected was her grandson, about to cross a busy street down the road. She was in a real predicament! In an instant, she yelled to the kids, having them all sit down. She then rushed off to the corner as fast as she could, to meet up with the boy she thought was Patrick. As she got closer, Paula's mom could see that it *was* her grandson!

How incredibly scary! Paula said that her mom yelled out his name, and screamed, "Stop!" Patrick's response wasn't what you might expect. He waved to his grandma in excitement and then said "Hey Grandma," according to Paula.

Paula's mom got to Patrick before he crossed the busy street and grabbed him by the hand. She asked him what he was doing, trying to make sense of the situation, and trying to remain calm. When she got back to the other kids who were sitting and waiting, she sat Pat down too. As calmly as she could, she continued to ask him why he was walking home. Patrick explained that there was a substitute teacher at school. It was early dismissal, and she told them it was time to "go home." Patrick took the message quite literal.

There were lots of things left undone that day, contributing to the very dangerous situation. Paula said that her mom called her at work. She started with, "I don't want you to worry, everything is fine," Paula said. Then she learned the details of what had happened with Pat. She left work, went straight to the school, and she let them have a piece of her mind! No one called from the school, which meant no one noticed that Pat didn't make it to after-school program that day.

It was quite an ordeal.

239

Paula was a little upset with her dad as well. Patrick showed his mom the way he had walked home, which included *jaywalking.* It was the route he and Grandpa had taken when they walked home before, whoopsie!

Through this situation, it became evident to Paula that Patrick still took things extremely literal; despite making tremendous progress, and being in the after-school program for over a year now. When explaining things to Patrick, it still needed to be done in a very specific way. Even though he had a daily routine down, when the teacher said, "it's time to go home," he literally only heard, "go home".

Patrick almost making it all the way home on his own, was very scary to Paula. He imitated the same route Grandpa had shown him. In a sense, it was fortunate that he walked home with his grandfather, which he mentally referenced to get home in this situation. Still, it could have gone in a very different way. What if it had been a different instruction from the teacher, with more potential dangers? That's not something Paula likes to think about.

During the following summer going into fifth grade, the school boundaries changed. Patrick started at a new school. Paula hoped this time he'd receive more school support, especially to help him with his literal interpretation of what people say. Maybe it was time to seek a clinical diagnosis.

Everything Happens for A Reason

Patrick was a nail biter. He would frequently get infections, because he'd bite his nails too short. He'd also get really bad ear infections as a result. Paula says she thinks that had a lot to do with his fingers being in his mouth and around his face. This meant frequent visits to the pediatrician. Paula would express her concerns regarding Patrick's behavior most of the time, and the doctor continued to assure her that everything was fine; despite being labeled with autism in school now. Paula still trusted the doctor's opinion and didn't push for more. "I mean he's known him from when he was born," she said. It made it easy to stop looking for answers at times.

There was one time, Pat developed an infection on his fingers that needed to be treated right away. Paula called the doctor's office, and was told that their pediatrician was not in. They'd have to see the doctor at the urgent care. It was pretty bad, so Paula didn't hesitate.

The office was a little more kid friendly than his usual doctor's office. When it was time for Pat to be seen, the doctor introduced herself and shook Patrick's hand. He immediately told the doctor his name. Pat continued talking, as he tends to do, as the doctor was inspecting his fingers. She then said she was going to grab some things to clean his fingers, and also asked Paula to join her outside the room for a minute. Paula was a little confused, but she went, not really sure of what it was about. The doctor explained that she didn't want to be offensive. Being that she wasn't Pat's regular pediatrician, and was just pulling up his chart for the first time, Paula knew the doctor was taking a risk with what happened next. Paula said that the doctor asked her, "has he been diagnosed…with autism?" "Instantly, I wanted to hug her for seeing it, in like five minutes," Paula said. Paula was overwhelmed to say the least. She burst into tears, and the doctor gave her a moment.

The irony of how this encounter came about was incredible! Pat's very particular nail biting behavior, sent them to be seen at the urgent care by this specific doctor; someone who was obviously familiar with autism. She was able to see the signs of autism within minutes, compared to the prior eleven years, of his regular pediatrician's dismissals of Paula's concerns. Patrick had been working through the world, now a fifth-grader, with a condition that hadn't been recognized clinically. Wow! It wasn't a surprise, but a weight lifted. Paula couldn't get home fast enough to share this news with her mother. Everything was different now, Paula was different. If you remember, earlier on, she avoided this admission.

Similar to the feelings that overcome parents receiving the actual diagnosis of autism, Paula went through a slough of emotions too. She was grateful and immensely relieved. She cried, prayed, and talked to her parents about the findings. She questioned if she should have fought harder. She defended her own dismissals with the notion that "professionals", were the ones who dismissed her concerns, time and time again. She accepted that all the moments leading up to this particular encounter, happened just as they needed to. Her instinctive hunch was finally validated.

The doctor told Paula that after sending her referral for Pat to be assessed, it would likely take some time before getting a scheduled appointment. Paula now had no doubt that Patrick would be diagnosed with some form of autism. She eagerly waited for Pat's assessment.

Assessment & Diagnosis

Appointments were now being set up for Patrick. Paula and her parents had to travel to San Jose for Pat's assessment to be done. It was an all-day ordeal.

There were several professionals involved during the assessment. This was largely due to Pat being diagnosed at an older age. Paula mentioned that she was asked about information from when Pat was a baby, up until that point. Eleven years of history was being gathered.

The questionnaires and assessment suggested that Patrick had symptoms of *Asperger Syndrome*. When the results were finally in, Paula was eager to hear them. Patrick was clinically diagnosed with *autism spectrum disorder (ASD)*, after years of wondering. This would change some things, but never the way his family saw him.

Family

Everyone in the family thought Patrick was extremely well behaved. He kept to himself, not bothering anyone. You know kids now-a-days, always occupied on devices? Well, Patrick was no exception there. In fact, that's possibly what made it easier for him to "blend in" with everyone else. He would sit quietly and watch his videos. To everyone around him, Pat looked like any other kid. Paula's family *never* suspected autism. Autism, wasn't even a word in existence among most of them.

Coming from a large Hispanic family, Paula was very involved, and there was always some event going on. She'd always take Patrick with her to family gatherings, and again, no one seemed to pick up on any of his autism traits. It was missed. He was the quiet, good kid, busy on his iPad.

Paula feels that Patrick has benefited from being around a lot of people. Though he still struggles to carry on conversations with peers, he can hold conversations with adults. Pat has also learned to behave in ways that don't draw unnecessary attention to himself. Paula is happy that she kept him socialized, even though she didn't realize the significance of it, at the time. She encourages other parents to keep their kids socialized, as best as they can as well.

After the diagnosis, Paula was given names of different therapies and facilities, through CVRC.

She didn't really know what they were, or what they did, so she did like any curious mother would. She *googled* them! She still didn't really understand how therapies like *applied behavior analysis (ABA)* worked, and what all the acronyms meant. She decided to look into the best rated providers and started there.

Starting Services

What came next were lots of appointments. Patrick had 20 hours a week of back-to-back, school to therapy days. It altered everyone's schedules. It changed everyone's lives.

Patrick was on the higher functioning side of the spectrum. What did he think about all this change? Paula said that she had explained to him that he would be going to a kind of "tutoring", to help with things he struggled with in school, and that he would make friends. "I tried to make more of like a social… you're gonna meet more friends…you're gonna go on field trips, and I was trying to make it more fun, more of a positive for him," Paula said. She encouraged Pat, even though it was gonna be challenging, that he could do it! She says that at that time, she didn't think Pat knew anything was "wrong" or different about himself. He wasn't aware of his differences until he got to middle school. Seventh grade was a whole new ballgame.

Becoming Aware of His Differences

When Paula would take Pat and drop him off for ABA, she would often see kiddos with more severe challenges than her own son's. Some kids would have meltdowns in the parking lot before getting to the door of the center. Paula started noticing that Patrick had a puzzled look on his face. It was as if he was trying to understand why he was there. She remembers the look that said, "I don't think I belong here." Pat couldn't relate to the other kids there. He didn't understand why some of the children at ABA behaved the way they did.

There was a peer at the center, that had a tendency to talk in a high-pitched voice. Paula remembers Patrick asking the boy, "why are you talking like that?" It didn't make sense to him. It didn't quite make sense to Paula either. Was there a mistake made. Did Patrick really have autism?

Paula was having doubts now. She had to read and learn everything she could about autism, to find out for herself. Through her own research, it was affirmed that Pat's diagnosis was accurate. Paula also learned that even though her son had this diagnosis, her view was still very narrow. She only knew her son's "flavor" of autism.

Paula knew what she had to do. In order to help Patrick understand other children, she would have to draw from experiences he could relate to. Regarding the boy at the autism center, Paula tried using an example to help her son understand why his peer might be talking in a high-pitched voice. Patrick loves going to Disney Land, so Paula used that in her example. She explained to him, "You know how you really love going to Disney…you don't really like to read…but you'll read a book about Disney, because Disney makes you happy?" She continued, "That's just how that boy communicates, that makes him happy. You talk about Disney, and some people are like, I don't like Disney — stop." In response, Paula remembers Pat saying, "but I don't talk like that." Paula found herself in a pickle. She then said, "everyone is different, and it's okay to be different." This statement made better sense to Patrick. He appeared to understand at that point.

After being in programs and therapy for some time, Patrick now realizes that he is *somewhat* different. He doesn't necessarily see the similarities between himself and another person with autism. It would be especially difficult for him to believe someone more severely affected by their autism, has the same condition he does. One of Paula's greatest fears for Patrick entering high school, was him being different in ways bigger than what he perceived himself to be. She worried about how other kids would receive him. Would they be kind? Would they make him feel bad, or even bully him? She worried about what it would really be like for Pat.

Cellphone Time

Freshman year put the pressure on. Paula had decided that she wouldn't buy a cell phone for Patrick, until he was at least sixteen years old. He went everywhere with his mom or grandparents, and he didn't have any real need for a phone. He had applications on his iPad, that could do just about anything a cellphone could do.

Paula took Pat to school for his freshman orientation. Sometime while they were there, the teacher suggested that Patrick take a picture of his class schedule with his phone. Paula paused for a minute, then explained to the teacher that Pat didn't have a cell phone. She felt the ice cold stare; a look of utter shock and judgement, from the teacher. Paula thought, "oh great,… here we go." It was made known that most of the students there had cell phones. On the way home Patrick made a smug remark, "if you would've just bought me a cell phone…" Paula remembers hearing him say.

Patrick got a phone for Christmas the year he turned sixteen. He did make it known that it *wasn't* the phone he wanted. Paula, also made it known, that *this* was the only phone he was getting from Santa! I'm sure Santa wasn't Patrick's favorite that year. At least he could download some cool apps on his new phone.

Social Media Apps

Patrick uses the application called *SnapChat*. Paula figured, "well he doesn't post too much, we should be fine." Come to find out, friends and family jokingly mentioned that because of Pat's posts, they always knew what the family was doing; where they were going, or where they were eating. Paula was just a little surprised. That's not all though, Patrick seemed to be enjoying this line of social media, and now he was asking to be allowed to have a *Facebook* or *Instagram* account on his phone. He had some pretty impressive arguments to persuade his mother, but Paula had the same answer, a firm "No". Patrick even reminded her that he was sixteen years old now, to which Paula responded, "thank you for that." Paula thinks that one social media outlet is enough at this time.

Self-Regulation

Patrick tends to want to please everyone, Paula says. He's a social kid, but when it comes to having actual friends and engaging in peer-social interactions, they are still working on that today. At school, the environment has eased Paula's mind somewhat. It's an environment of positivity and inclusivity.

Pat gets along with most of his peers, but there was one student that he wasn't quite the best of friends with. "There's always that one kid for everyone," Paula says. Pat had one school peer that would always try to "one up" him in a sense. It was an odd rivalry. Paula said, "I would have to tell him to let it go, and this was before Frozen the movie came out!" She would instruct Pat to take a deep breath, and let it go, any time he was upset about something. With tools like this, Patrick is learning to *self-regulate*. Even though he's considered "high functioning", he still requires this kind of support.

Social Awkwardness

Say Hi Pat

Through the years, Patrick got used to either being home or at family functions. He also regularly goes to stores and shops with his family. There have been times where he's run into classmates from school at a store who tell him "hi", but he doesn't consistently say it back. Paula has tried explaining to him, that it's polite to respond. Pat sometimes insists that he's already responded. Sometimes, he says "hi" in response to his mom's instruction, but by the time he does, the person is already gone.

Good Manners

At one family function, one of Paula's aunts was sitting nearby. She started sneezing and coughing, and Patrick immediately said, "God bless you." He continued by asking if she was okay or needed water. This made an impression on that aunt. Paula says, her aunt always remembers him as a sweet, well mannered kid. That's kind of how he is with most adults, Paula shared.

It's not the same with other kids and his peers. Pat can make a definite impression on the adults though.

Fun Facts About Patrick

Even though other kids aren't his cup of tea, there is some childhood magic known to many, that captivates Patrick. Patrick loves Disney and Sesame Street. He also loves Pasta, but he does not like food from Dicicco's Italian restaurant, according to Paula. At Dicicco's, Paula has discovered that the smell of the herbs bother Pat. Also, he has decided that he's, "allergic to Mexican food," Paula said. She found herself thinking of a good way to break it to him, that being allergic to something and not liking it, are very different things. She had to tell him that he wasn't "allergic" to an entire food type.

Patrick likes dancing. He is a bit of a social butterfly, Paula mentioned, despite the difficulties he faces in making friends. He's eager to be a part of activities and to get involved with lots of things.

Confident Pat

Patrick wants to do everything that interests him. "I don't want to say, like do everything 'normal kids' can," Paula continued, "but he wants to do — everything," she said. For example, he can swim okay, but he thinks he's a swimmer. He wants to be on the swim team at school. He's extremely confident, but "Im not gonna take him out to a lake to go swimming," Paula said. He wants to play water polo now, but doesn't know how to play the game, and he's not the best swimmer. The team offer is to make Pat a "manager" or "coach", but that's not what he wants. Pat wants what every other kid on the water polo team wants, to play. Paula had to say no, due to his overconfidence about his swimming abilities, and his inability to see his differences the way others do. As another demonstration of Pat's overconfidence, paula said, "he has an A in P.E., so he thinks he's athletic."

Just like other parents, Paula wants her son to be invited to participate in something completely, not just in a minimal way. There are other things that Pat can participate better in. His overconfidence, doesn't help these situations.

Bike Riding

Patrick wants to ride his bike 3 to 4 miles home. Paula wont allow him to, even though she believes he can technically do it. Her concern is Patrick's safety. To this day, he does a tunnel vision thing, where he doesn't turn his head to check for traffic when he gets to the corner of a street. He uses his peripheral vision, and only looks out of the corners of his eyes. Paula knew it was a bit strange when he was younger. She didn't worry too much about it, since he was always with an adult on walks (with the exception of the time he walked home by himself in elementary school). Nonetheless, because of the odd way he checks for traffic, it's incredibly unsafe for Pat to ride his bike home alone. Cars might not pay attention to him in that turning lane, and he might miss the cars in his odd check, thinking it's safe to cross the street. Despite this concern, Patrick insists that he can do it. It's a sore subject, but Paula just cannot agree to it. I don't blame her one bit. Regardless of the reason, Paula knows this is frustrating for Patrick.

The struggle is real for Paula! She doesn't want to diminish Patricks confidence in any way; but as his parent, she has the responsibility to keep her son safe. Pat struggles with deciphering between unrealistic expectations, and realistic outcomes, due to his overconfidence. Paula wants to root him on, but she doesn't want to encourage the overconfidence. She tries to let him be as independent and involved as possible, within reason.

To help lessen Pat's overconfidence, Paula has a few people in her life that try to teach Patrick about the results of hard work and consistency. Pat's grandpa plays a huge role here. Grandpa is a little old fashioned, and does things a little different than Paula; some good, and some not so great.

Grandpa; the Buddy, Father Figure, & Model

Paula shared that Patrick and his grandpa are best buds. Grandpa is the father figure in Patrick's life. Although, he doesn't seem to understand the little considerations required of Pat's autism. For instance, regarding a multi-step task he wanted Pat to complete, Paula told her dad "no, he can only do two of those six tasks you want him to do." These kinds of corrections have been met with responses like, "he knows what he's doing." Paula has stressed to her parents, that if her father shows Patrick how to do certain things, and maybe even repeat himself a few times, Pat will get the hang of it. It just takes him more time, and a little more effort to learn. It also takes more patience on their part. Paula is confident, with that recipe, Patrick can do almost anything. If the task is modeled, then taught step-by-step, Patrick is likely to remember every part, and eventually be able to do it all on his own.

Throwing out the Trash

One day Paula asked Patrick to throw out the trash. There is a key needed to unlock the gate where the trash bins are. Patrick told Paula that he couldn't do it, because he didn't know *how* to throw out the trash. He also mumbled something about needing a key, so Paula said, "well go get the key." Patrick then told her that he didn't know where to get the key. A huge epiphany, if you will, came over Paula. Her son has brought the bathroom trash to the kitchen bin to empty it there. Grandpa handles the rest. Grandpa comes from a generation and culture, where young men are just "supposed" to know how to take care of things, like throwing out the trash. Paula shared that her father is also the person that will just, "handle it himself," if something isn't done. He was completing the remainder of the task of throwing out the trash. This left Patrick to believe that there wasn't anything else for him to do. He'd bring the bathroom trash to the kitchen bin, and every day it was somehow empty.

In life, when Patrick is out of their "bubble", as Paula says, grandpa will not be there to handle the rest. This meant that Patrick needed to learn how to complete this seemingly simple, yet complex task. It became more and more evident to Paula while modeling and explaining every step (down to "roll out garbage bin to the curb"), that Pat had never done anything remotely laborious in his life! As she realized this, she also recognized the need to teach him so many other things. Throwing out the trash was only one of many steps, in Pat's road to becoming self-sufficient. Doing things for him, was NOT in his best interest.

When talking to Patrick about this, he tried like any teen would, to weasel his way out. He'd say stuff like, "well I'll be going to college,'"according to Paula. He acted as if that made it irrelevant to follow through on chores. Grandma was quick as a whip, and would then ask questions like,"who will wash your clothes?" and "who will make your food?" They started working on those life-skills, despite Patrick's lack of enthusiasm.

With a little coaching, Pat could do things like; make a sandwich by himself, or heat up something in the microwave. He was more capable than he knew. Paula knew this, and so did Grandma, and so they've continued to push him, simply because, he *is* capable.

There was no denying that Patrick was growing up. He started wanting what most teens want. He wanted a little more freedom and independence. This also meant, more responsibilities for Patrick. Interestingly, getting a child with autism to initiate and become independent, is what most parents strive for. This is something many parents of children with special needs only dream of actually happening. Independence now looked very achievable in Pat's future.

A Special Kind of Prom

Patrick wanted to be involved in school activities, as mentioned before. Paula pushed him to be involved in things outside of school as well. She wanted to provide her son with more opportunities to help him overcome his social struggles.

Every year, there is a prom put on by community
agencies for kids and young adults with special needs.
Paula had submitted the application for Patrick to
participate in the event, without him knowing. She
received a congratulatory message, inviting Patrick to
attend the event. Paula was so excited! Then she thought,
"oh sh**, how am I gonna tell him?" She was a nervous
wreck, also realizing that she wasn't going to be in town
on the date of the event, yikes! Paula said, "I was like
sweeting bullets." She had no idea how Patrick was
going to react to the news.

A First Time for Everything

Paula told her mom about the prom. Grandma
was certain it would be fine, being that Patrick loves
dancing. Paula wasn't too sure about that. "Okay mom,
you're gonna have to sit here with me when I tell him,"
she said to her mom. So later that day, they sat down
with Pat. Paula pulled up the Facebook page of the event
to show him. She remembers Patrick saying, "It's a
prom..but it's not my school prom." She thought this was

her window in; a moment to talk up the event, and get
Pat all excited about it! "Yeah it's not your prom, but it's
for kids your age and older, and they have autism, and
other disabilities…and it's okay to be different..," she
said. Before she could get another word in, Patrick told
her that he planned to go to prom the following year, his
junior year. Paula replied, "yeah okay…but this is like a
practice run..," and she was shocked with what followed!
Patrick interrupted her, and adamantly told her, "no!"
Then, almost shouting, Pat said to his mom, "I'm not
going!" Paula was extremely surprised by her son's
response, and it didn't stop there.

Patrick had never stood his ground like this
before. This teenager had never objected like this before
to something his mom brought to the table. Paula
described the serious look on Pat's face, as he asked her,
"are you going to force me to go?" She couldn't believe
her eyes, or ears! Paula and Grandma were in shock.

Paula told Patrick that they needed to have a
discussion. She started with, " Look, you are fifteen,"

then Pat interjected with, "almost sixteen," with a bit of an eye roll. Paula continued, "we take you lots of different places, and you try lots of different things, and what do we say? You have to try it once." Pat still seemed appalled at the idea. He was suddenly sharp with come-backs for everything his mother was explaining to him.

Secretly, Paula was really proud of her son for standing his ground. Now was not the time to let him know she liked this new side of him though. Not when he was resisting her efforts to convince him that this prom would be a good experience for him. Paula had to take the reins. She explained all the details including; who was gonna take Pat, what he was gonna wear, and what it would be like.

Paula then told Patrick that he needed to get ready, because they had to go get him fitted for a tuxedo. Again, she pulled from a wedding experience, for Pat to reference what getting fitted for a tuxedo meant. Patrick then reluctantly made his way to take a shower, taking a whole three minutes. Teenagers! Then, when he was ready to go, he made sure to let his mom know that he had thought about it. Pat agreed to go to the prom, but declared that he "wouldn't have any fun!" Paula says that he was worried about not knowing anyone there. She tried to convince him that he might run into people he knew from school, or make new friends while there.

Through the process, Paula made sure to remind Patrick that everything he was doing, is what he'd do when he went to his school's "real" prom. Pat wasn't any happier about the whole situation, despite his mother's efforts. She tried to make tuxedo fitting fun. She tried to pump him up with name dropping, "B-95" as the entertainment host for the evening. She tried and tried, and nonetheless, Patrick was certain that it would…suck. He was hung up on thinking he wouldn't know anyone at the event.

The Experience

To his surprise, and Paula's too, everything went great at prom! Patrick had a wonderful time. What? How could this be, when he didn't know anyone there? Well, as it turned out Patrick was paired up with a student volunteer. He was initially paired up with a male student. Something happened, and the volunteers needed to switch, and then Pat was paired with a female student volunteer. Paula thought it might have been awkward for him to be paired with a girl, but instead, Patrick was thrilled to meet someone from another school! He also saw some other kids from his own school there, as well as some volunteers that he was already familiar with. Patrick was grinning from ear to ear, the entire night, as reported by his grandma to Paula. Paula's parents where impressed with how well the event was coordinated. The volunteers, the students, the red carpet, and decor; all of it was a truly magical experience, in their opinions.

When Paula recapped on the event with Patrick, he confirmed everything her parents had already told her. Pat shared with his mom that he wanted to go back next year. Paula was excited to hear this! Then, in traditional Patrick style, he said that he wanted to go back next year, as a *volunteer*. There it was, a great experience, with a side of his extreme confidence. Patrick knew exactly what role he'd stand his ground for next time.

Paula has learned to love her son's confidence. They're working on his *overconfidence*. Even though it can cause friction sometimes, she thinks his confidence is more of a positive trait. She wants him to continue aspiring to reach new goals with that confidence.

Should've, Would've, Could've

Like many parents of kiddos with special needs, Paula is familiar with the, "I should've, would've, could've," song. Paula said, " I should've been a little more vocal, and I should've been a better advocate for him. Not that I didn't fight, but I just feel that I could've put up a better fight." Now looking back and seeing other people, and actually knowing what autism could look like; very similar, yet so different, it stings just a little for Paula. She knows that she did the best she could at that time. Knowing now that he could have had the diagnosis of autism earlier on, perhaps if she would've fought harder, hurts a bit. Again, looking back at the early years with her son, when they got that speech delay diagnosed, Paula remembers thinking, "this is it, we've got that!" She felt proactive and productive then.

If she could do it all again, Paula would have questioned more, and demanded a little bit more for her son. She had put her trust in the "professionals". She trusted her son's doctor with everything. Paula added, "The doctors are the one's you think should know, and know it all." It became evident that Patrick's doctor didn't really know about autism.

Excuses Maybe

Paula admits to looking for excuses for Pat's behavior many times. For example, he went from Head Start with a more one-to-one environment, where he did great, to preschool which wasn't the easiest for him. In preschool, there were thirty kids, one teacher, and the classroom assistant. Paula used to think that explained why he was clamming up, and not wanting to talk.

She normalized all of his behavior.

She didn't know the impact minimizing it would have in the long run. Paula was like many special-needs parents, looking for something to explain her son's behavior, but avoiding a label. Perhaps subconsciously avoiding facing the "problem". Maybe not wanting the "I told you so", fear of the unknown, and just plainly not wanting this "autism" for her son, strengthened and rationalized the excuses. Paula also admits that there came a point when school became more challenging, and things started to surface that weren't worked on before. This is when the excuses stopped working.

The pivotal moments along this journey have provided Paula with an abundance of knowledge. She is happy that her son is at the level he's at today. Despite not getting him diagnosed until later, the things she's continually worked on with him, (since before the diagnosis) have made a difference. Patrick has work to do before he's fully independent, but he's getting a little closer every day.

What Autism Means to This Mom

It's just a word. It's not a label she uses to introduce him with, in her life. With lots of family and friends, no one has ever openly questioned if he has autism. "It's not like a disease, it's not like a death sentence," Paula added. She says that when you get to know him, you might think he's a little different, but that's about it.

Life Without Autism

Paula would not cure Patrick's autism if it were an option. Her rational is very interesting to me, and insightful! Paula thinks, because of the world we live in today, people are very disconnected. Autism makes it necessary for her family to have more in-depth conversations about everything. That part wouldn't be there if her son's autism was gone. Patrick might be like other teens across the nation. He'd likely be even more absorbed in technology, on a phone all day, if it weren't for his autism. To actually have the communication however different it is, is a rare commodity, and something she wouldn't change.

Advice to Other Parents

Paula encourages others to learn from her mistakes and experiences overall. "Go with your gut," Paula stresses. She believes that if she would have done the same earlier on, she might have been able to work on things, that she is just now needing to work on with Patrick. Even at work, she advises co-workers to follow their gut. If something doesn't feel right, ask questions and get to the bottom of things, she says. Autism isn't the end of the world, according to Paula. Even though Pat didn't get diagnosed with autism until he was older, she's never stopped fighting for him. She encourages parents to pay attention to everything in their child's development.

Autism has taught Paula to be a little more open minded. She's learned to think outside the box, and to become accepting of everything. The truth is, every day *isn't* the greatest, in her journey with autism.

She has learned to be more patient because of that. For Paula, a big factor is ACCEPTANCE.

There have been many times where she'd like to see something change in Patrick, and so they work tirelessly on those things. Sometimes despite their efforts, she has to *accept* things as they are — she has to be okay with that. "The next day is a new day, you kind of just start over, and it's okay," Paula said. All the wins are wins! The one thing that she will not bend on however, is getting Patrick to shower — EVERYDAY! That fight, may very well just be a teen boy thing. All fact, no excuses.

It's not always easy to come to terms with the diagnosis, no matter what age your child is. Paula and I agree that it's important for people raising children with autism, to find their support community. Paula also realizes that she still doesn't know everything about autism, and can always learn more. This holds true no matter where you are on the this journey. Lastly, Paula encourages and reminds us that, "we can always do better, we can always learn."

My Take

This story made me smile a few times. Paula's description of her son Patrick, is phenomenal! Paula's story is unique, in that she went without an official diagnosis for her son for quite some time. I think she did a fabulous job of still working with her son, and trying to get him support, even without the diagnosis.

One of the main points that stood out to me, is how dismissive the pediatrician was for several years. I have heard from other parents, and even some of the other stories in this book have mentioned, how doctors dismiss concerns regarding autism. I think it's unfortunate that we learn about red flags that warrant concern, and then when we try to bring it to the table, it gets shut down! What is a parent to do then? It appears to me that advocacy starts even before a diagnosis often times. Even still, many parents of children with ASD tend to find out after searching for long periods of time, that what describes their child's condition, is what they've suspected all along. It's ultimately autism.

275

Another unique consideration Paula talked about, was teaching her son how to take care of things that matter in life. Taking out the trash and taking a shower, were some of the examples she mentioned. I often get caught up in the educational piece, and don't get me wrong, that is super important. Then, I realize that there's still life-skills that need to be taught to my son. Education matters, but life-skills will allow my son to conduct himself in a somewhat "normal" manner day in and day out. It's really easy to get in a habit of doing everything for your special-needs kids. We might be doing more harm than good, if we don't provide them the guidance and allow them the independence, to reach their full potential.

Lastly, Paula's story demonstrates the importance of giving things a try, at least once. This is a notion suited specifically for our community. Parents of children with autism have a lot on their plate. Expending unnecessary energy, often becomes part of our check and balance system. Trying new things is 100 percent, worth the energy, in my opinion. You'll get the opportunity to see if something works or doesn't.

CHAPTER 9

A Greater Purpose

It's always fun running into old friends and learning about where their life has taken them. Most of us with kids, have one or two around the same age. When my son was four years old and we were new to navigating a life with special needs, I crossed paths with an old high school friend, Julia. As it turned out, she was navigating through a similar kind of life.

Julia's son has special needs. He's a few years older than my son with autism. I was happy to learn all I could about what things she was using with her boy, to see if those techniques would work for mine. For a short period of time, Julia served as a board member for Fresno Autism Network (FAN), the organization I founded. Over the years we've kept in touch. We talk every now and then, especially when there's an event or something related to autism happening.

It's fascinating to see how each of our boys have grown in their own stories with special needs.

Julia is a preschool teacher for children with special needs. She and her husband Gilbert, have four children together; three girls and one boy. Their son Timothy is the eldest of his sibling. He has Autistic-like traits.

About Timothy

Timothy is fifteen years old. He's clinically diagnosed with *attention deficit hyper activity disorder (ADHD), mood disorder*, and *disruptive behavior disorder*. At two years old, he was assessed through the *Central Valley Regional Center (CVRC)*. It was thought that he "might" have autism. Half a year later, Timothy was diagnosed with *mixed expressive receptive language disorder*. Eventually that diagnosis was removed. How can one child embody so many conditions? Well, let's start from the beginning.

Welcome to the World Timothy

Timothy was was born almost six weeks early. He had to stay in the hospital for a few days for his lungs to get stronger. When they would touch his skin, Julia says that he would get overstimulated, and start breathing rapidly. For this reason, they had to refrain from holding him for the first few days. Other than that, Julia took all the precautions an expectant mother should.

"I didn't dye my hair..I wasn't a coffee drinker back then…I didn't go into the salon. I took my prenatals," Julia said. She did everything she was supposed to be doing while pregnant. It was a normal pregnancy.

Moving forward, Julia specifically remembers holding Timothy when he was an infant. She was breastfeeding him in her room in the one bedroom apartment they had at that time. She remembers thinking, "he's going to be the kid that everyone likes." She thought he'd be the softball player in preschool, the kid the teacher likes, and that he'd be popular.

"I'm gonna dress him like this, and put this on him.. little shorts, and a little hat..and he's gonna go to school, and just be so smart, and everyone's gonna love him," Julia remembered thinking. She saw him as a happy boy that everyone would love! She also saw him as athletic, like his daddy.

The Long Road Through Diagnosis

When Timothy was still a baby, Julia started noticing some differences in her son. She noticed that his younger cousin was on track, meeting all the developmental milestones you read about. Timothy, on the other hand, was a little behind. His cousin was only three months younger, so Julia didn't think too much of this discrepancy at first. In fact, when her nephew would do something new, she was excited. She thought this meant her son was going to be doing that same thing very soon.

When Timothy was a year old, Julia and her husband were thrilled to hear his first real word!

He started saying "dad" any time he saw Gilbert. This was truly exciting for these parents!

Timothy's cousin's development continued progressing. His vocabulary grew, and he'd follow directions. He'd point to his mouth or nose when asked to do so, for example. He was now saying about five words, and Timothy remained with only his one word. Julia's nephew continued progressing; making eye contact, responding to his own name, and more. However, her son still wasn't doing any of that! Her nephew would play with multiple toys, but Timothy wouldn't. He only had one toy or thing, that he was interested in. At twenty one months old, just shy of turning two, Julia noticed that Timothy *stopped* saying, "dad". Now, not only was Julia's nephew ahead of Timothy in reaching milestones, but Timothy was going backward it seemed.

At that time, Julia started to notice similarities in Timothy and another cousin of his. This cousin was older and had autism.

This cousin wouldn't respond to his name. Julia and her husband, saw how his parents would try to get his attention by calling his name, with no success. It scared Julia to recognize that her little boy wasn't responding to his own name either.

After thinking about it, she wanted to test it out agin. She told Gilbert, "call him." She was hoping to get Timothy to respond when they called his named. So Gilbert did. Timothy didn't respond. Every time they'd try to get Timothy's attention by calling his name, he would not respond. Putting all these pieces together, Julia now suspected something was very wrong with her little boy. Did he have the same condition his older cousin had?

Julia took Timothy to the doctor, and similar to the theme of the previous chapters, her concerns were dismissed. Julia remembers the doctor saying, "he's fine, nothing's wrong. He'll get it, he's a boy." Julia knew that something was very wrong.

Timothy lost his only word, he wasn't babbling, and he wasn't pointing at things he wanted. "he would scream…" Julia said. She didn't know what he needed or wanted, which meant she didn't know how to help calm her son. He wouldn't lead her by the hand to show her, like a younger child might. There was definitely a communication barrier. Julia was at a loss.

Julia *needed* help for her son, so she went back to his doctor. Before returning to the doctor, someone along the way had told her to emphasize the word "regression", when expressing her concerns. Julia took this advice seriously. If nothing else, she made it a point to say "regression", during her visit to Timothy's doctor. She explained that the one word he had, "dad" — was gone. She also told the doctor about the other things she was noticing in her son. This time, the doctor made a referral for Timothy to CVRC. Here he would be assessed for autism, and other developmental delays. This happened right before Timothy turned two.

"I think it was by the grace of God, that they got me in right away," Julia added. It's no secret to the special-needs community, that getting an assessment done at CVRC, can sometimes be a lengthy wait. They definitely got lucky with that one!

Timothy didn't meet all the criteria to be diagnosed with *autism spectrum disorder (ASD)*, but it was still suspected. Being that he was only two years old, he was sent to receive services at *Exceptional Parents Unlimited (EPU)*, with a provisional diagnosis of autism. The clinicians wanted to see how much he developed in a year's time. At three years old, they would re-evaluate him to see if he met the criteria for autism then, or any other condition.

When he turned three years old, Timothy was re-evaluated at CVRC. He was given a diagnosis, but not of autism. The doctor said that he was just shy of meeting the criteria for an autism diagnosis. This was a little concerning to Julia at the time, but Timothy did receive a diagnosis of, *mixed expressive receptive language disorder.*

Initially, before receiving his first official clinical diagnosis, CVRC had told Julia that Timothy might have autism, as mentioned earlier. She remembers when that happened, walking out of CVRC, and balling her eyes out! She had only a limited view of autism back then which was that of her nephew who is Autistic, and her own cousin. Her cousin's severe condition made that view an extremely bleak one. She was terrified of that reality for her son! Her cousin was already older, completely nonverbal, hand flapping and making loud vocal sounds, among other things. That's what Julia thought Timothy would grow to be like. It broke her heart. This was nowhere near what she wanted her son to be. One of Julia's biggest fears was not knowing what was going to happen to him. She didn't know where to turn for help.

Fix Him

The next phase for Julia, was an overwhelming need to "fix" her son. She recalls thinking, "Okay fix him, so I can have that kid that I want." She continued to explain that she knew it sounded awful, but she was desperate for them to "get on with their lives," she said. Julia kept going back to thinking that Timothy was going to be just like her cousin. She tried to come to terms with the fact that he was never gonna talk. The thought would replay in her mind over and over again.

When he got the diagnosis of *mixed expressive receptive language disorder*, there was a small sigh of relief. Julia now knew that there was potential for Timothy to start talking again, with the right kind of help. She still knew however, that there was more going on with him. She wished that the doctor who diagnosed him in 30 minutes, would come to her home, and see ALL of Timothy. Then the doctor would see the way he would melt down, scream, stuff food in his cheeks, go to bed with food in his mouth, and hold on to that toy dinosaur he had. "I can't even tell you what it was like, how many times…I mean he had to go to school..He couldn't give it up," Julia added, regarding Timothy's favorite dinosaur toy. She felt defeated and overwhelmed. There was so much more that needed attention, but it wasn't part of the diagnosis he received.

With the new diagnosis, came more questions. She was even more confused about Timothy's future now. She knew all those behaviors she wished the doctor could see, *needed* attention! What was the best thing for her to do? Julia's husband hugged her and told her that everything would be alright. Even still, she wasn't sure exactly how it would be alright.

The Blame Game

A common question that parents and family members have when a child is diagnosed with some condition is, "Why?" Julia experienced this as well. She remembers her own mom saying that she didn't take all her prenatal vitamins. Almost suggesting that was the cause of all of Timothy's challenges. Julia says, "it's a very old way of thinking." She wasn't sure if that way of thinking is only in her culture or family, but suspects it's not. From all the stories I've heard, I can say her suspicions are correct! That type of thinking happens more often than I care to admit.

Vaccines Maybe

For a little while, Julia herself, tried to understand how her son did end up with these conditions. She explored the vaccine injury theory, but not until after she had already gone through with his early series of immunizations. She later had a delayed schedule of vaccines done with her daughter, because honestly, she was a little scared. Her other daughters however, got their vaccines on time. They don't display any characteristics of autism, or any of the other conditions Timothy is diagnosed with. She shifted her focus onto being proactive when she couldn't find any real answers.

First Words Again

Timothy's first word was "dad", as mentioned earlier, but he stopped saying that. He had become nonverbal. His teacher from EPU, Jessica, would bring play dough to the home sessions, to work on gross and fine motor skills, as well as language. She would put the play dough on the table and start rolling it out, saying, "roll, roll, roll," Julia explained. Timothy wouldn't say anything, and would appear to just want to play. One time, Julia was sitting at the table while the EPU teacher was going through the same routine with Timothy. Julia said, "I remember, he was wearing a red little shirt, and she said, 'roll, roll, roll,' and he looks at her, and he goes, 'ro - ro - ro.'" No way! Julia was in disbelief and thrilled to hear her son's sweet little voice saying a real word again! She became eager to have him say it again, and to say other words too. Julia explained how she used that same little phrase for other things she wanted Timothy to say. She'd say "cup, cup, cup", when trying to get him to say the word "cup" for example. At almost three years old Timothy was starting to talk. This was quite a miracle! His language skills started developing little by little. At four years old, he started talking in complete three-word sentences. Julia thought that everything was going to be fine now that Timothy could speak. However, Timothy still wasn't able to regulate his emotions. As he entered public school, he started having behavioral difficulties.

The Fight Begins

The experience with EPU was phenomenal, as Julia recalls. The teacher that would come to the house and work with Timothy was amazing. Even before he had an official diagnosis, everything with EPU was extremely interactive, and helped Timothy a lot. After receiving the *mixed expressive receptive language disorder* diagnosis through CVRC, in home *ABA* services were started. However, the service offered didn't meet Julia's expectation.

The company that was assigned to the family, didn't make a good impression, to say the least.

They would make appointments with the family, then not show up. They were doing a *consultation model*, but nothing was modeled or described clearly. Here Julia was studying to be a teacher, and she was having a hard time understanding how ABA worked. She was provide only a minimal amount of information by the therapist. The report from the provider wasn't even Timothy's! When it was sent over to the CVRC social worker, Julia was informed that there was another child's name on it! Can you believe that? What other pertinent information was incorrect? On top of all that, it was just a few months shy of Timothy's CVRC eligibility being terminated, since he didn't have a qualifying disability there. He would transition to the local school district for early preschool and services.

Julia got a glimpse of her future. If getting her son good quality early intervention services was difficult, she realized she was in for a long fight. She recognized that things weren't gonna come easy. She had to get prepared for what was yet to come in school, and she could only image what all of that entailed.

Timothy did horribly for his assessment going into preschool, Julia explained. As she recalls, he lay flat on the floor during the assessment. She suspected that he wasn't going to do well, and probably wouldn't score on a lot of things, but she didn't expect that he'd lay on the ground the entire time. He was still considered nonverbal at that time as well. This didn't reflect any of what Timothy could do. It didn't help his case too much. It reminded me a lot of my own son during many assessments in school. The boy is capable, but he'd have you think otherwise.

After the assessment, they were led to a little room where they discussed the results. It's a bittersweet feeling for Julia, because she works at the same school where Timothy had his assessment done. She now sits in on *IEP's* as a teacher, sometimes in that same room, where her son's educational plan all started. It's also the same room where Timothy received yet another label.

293

Another Label

Another blow was tacked on that same year when Timothy was getting ready to enter preschool. He was given the label of *mental retardation* by the school. Julia had an extremely difficult time accepting that label. Julia's perception of what that label meant, was based on a cousin of her's in Mexico. He would rock back and forth in a corner, and no one paid attention to him. When she was little, she remembered her aunt telling everyone to just leave him alone.

It's a very tough pill to swallow for many parents of kiddos with special needs. You find yourself wondering if you missed something, or if they've got it wrong. Then, when you can see your child's potential (when others are blinded by their deficits), you start to believe that they probably don't have it right. You could talk until you're blue in the face, but there's just no way to force them to see through your eyes.

There is a taboo surrounding the term "mental retardation". The "r" word, as our community refers to it, isn't something to be taken lightly. Today, you might hear people loosely throw around the "r" word, as an insult or pun. However, to those who's children have the condition, or are labeled with it, it's hurtful and not funny at all. The term carries the stigma, that those with the label are "dumb" or "stupid". According to Michelle Diament, with Disability Scoop, an online news source, the bill for federal agencies to make the change of using "Intellectual Disability", in place of "Mental Retardation", was signed by President Obama in 2010. This bill was called, Rosa's Law, named after a girl with Down Syndrome. Diament says the change was initiated in an effort to remove the use of hurtful language in policy, by those agencies involved in providing support to individual's with special needs (Disability Scoop, 2010). It would take years before the change was made across the nation. The term change hadn't happened in Timothy's school yet.

What is Mental Retardation/Intellectual Disability?

According to an article by Anand K. Srivastava and Charles E. Schwartz, 70 percent of children with autism also had an intellectual disability (2014). "intellectual disability" is a condition characterized by below average intellectual functioning (IQ<70) in conjunction with significant limitations in adaptive functioning" (Srivastava & Charles, 2014).

This label didn't sit right with Julia, and she felt that it was inaccurate. Timothy's speech therapist attended the next IEP to discuss classroom placement options for him, "Oh I love her, from EPU,"Julia said. At the meeting, the speech therapist looked at Julia. She pointed to that label on the paperwork, and Julia remembers her saying, "look…no…but keep it on there so he could get his services." Timothy qualified for special-education services with this label, and so he was able to be placed in a *special day classroom (SDC)*.

When Timothy's clinical diagnosis was changed, the school removed the label of "mental retardation".

In first grade, the primary diagnosis that impeded on his learning, was then considered ADHD. Julia was content with this decision, and Timothy still qualified for his IEP.

Around the time Timothy was five years old, there was another doctor that told Julia, Timothy had tendencies of Autism, but not enough to be diagnosed with the condition. After that time, Timothy's behaviors started getting really bad. Since autism was dismissed clinically, the school didn't jump on assessing Timothy for it. Also, because he already had an IEP with ADHD listed as the primary thing impeding on his learning, coupled with his other diagnoses, the school went with that.

The Hidden Depression

One of the hardest things for Julia was having to see Timothy struggle in school, and become depressed during his early school years. She doesn't know when he became depressed, but she remembers when she found out. During first grade, Timothy started coming home from school "screaming and crying saying he wanted to die," Julia said. Timothy was referred to *Comprehensive Youth Services (CYS)* through the school district. He started seeing a therapist there. Timothy was having severe *meltdowns* at school and at home.

One day Timothy was in the kitchen at home, and Julia remembers him saying, "I'm gonna get a knife, and I'm gonna slice my ear off!" Julia discreetly started recording the incident to show his therapist. She remembered some of what she had worked on with the therapist, for instance, not feeding into the behavior, and making sure Timothy was safe. He couldn't find a knife so he got a fork and Julia remembers, "he was screaming, 'I'm gonna slice my face!'"she said. He was a first-grader! She didn't understand how this little person could behave this way, or why he was feeling that way. She was emotionally overwhelmed. Julia sternly told him that he was *not* going to slice his face, and that he needed to put the fork down. She reminded him, "we love you," she said. Timothy finally put the fork down.

Julia was terrified about what the future would be like for her son now, with all this. Was he going to be a sociopath? At the time he was hitting others at school, running out of class, and now making threats to hurt himself. She didn't know what to do. I can't even image what that must have felt like!

After that experience, his therapist did an exercise, having Timothy draw a picture of himself at school. He drew a picture with a slide and a few kids together, and one kid by himself. The therapist asked Timothy to tell her about the picture. Julia remembers the therapist telling her what Timothy said, while pointing to the kid by himself in his drawing. "That's me over here, because no one wants to play with me, because I'm the bad kid," she said. Julia broke down. The therapist told her that Timothy was depressed. It was a really hard time for Julia, and flooded with pain only a mother could know.

The Rollercoaster:Phases

For Julia, all of the diagnoses and labels, were one blow after another over the years. It was mentally draining and emotionally exhausting for her. Julia's life with special needs has been a rollercoaster. She went through phases throughout the years of wondering who her son would be. When he was nonverbal, and continually melting down, she thought he was gonna be like her nephew with autism. She thought that he was never gonna talk. When he was given the label of *mental retardation*, she thought he would end up like her cousin in Mexico, rocking in the corner forever! Then he started talking, and her perspective shifted to a more hopeful one. Then, he started hitting people, and saying he was going to kill himself. At that time she wondered, "is he going to be a serial killer?" All of this triggered immense anxiety in Julia. Any time the phone rang she'd expected the worst. Would it be another problem with Timothy?

"You're just kind of going through life. You're like, what can I deal with, and what can I take on," Julia

300

explained regarding her emotional and mental position at that time. She didn't know what the difference would be if she fought for an autism label at school. Was it even worth it? She was overwhelmed with her son's depression. At that time she was pregnant with her third child, so pushing for a different assessment wasn't even something she was looking to do. So, she decided to go with what was right in front of them for the time being. It was a lot to handle. "The school from my point of view, if they already have something, they'll go with that...it makes it easier," Julia said regarding what qualified him for an IEP. She also notices this happening today, with students in her own classroom.

Julia's Heart Says He's On The Autism Spectrum, No Label Needed

The early school years where incredibly difficult for the family. Timothy required a lot of support for his emotional, social and academic challenges. He acquired several diagnoses, and changes to existing ones throughout the early school years.

You might think that was a lot of diagnosis for one little boy to embody. Julia thought so. It seemed to her like something else could better account for all of the individual diagnosis her son was given. Julia says she remembers thinking, "could you just put him as having *PDD* and we'll be done with it? I mean all these things! Oh my goodness!" Julia really felt that *pervasive developmental disorder-not otherwise specified (PDD-NOS)*, was what her son had.

PDD-NOS or PDD, was one of the five different types of autism spectrum disorders, before changes were made to the diagnostic criteria and terminology. Now it would just be classified as *autism spectrum disorder (ASD)*. According to National Autism Resources, PDD-NOS was diagnosed when someone had some behaviors seen in autism, but not enough to meet the full criteria (2020).

Moving through the early elementary school years, time and time again, teachers and therapist agreed that Timothy had PPD-NOS. However, no one could tell

Julia exactly where to go to get that diagnosis, or how to get a re-evaluation done. She found herself stuck with what was on the paperwork in front of her, with no knowledge of how to fight it and have it changed. She did what she knew how to, and kept fighting for Timothy's success, as hard as it was to do.

There were numerous things that pointed to PDD in Timothy. First off, he had his speech delay, after initially having verbal language. He had sensory issues. He was what some professionals refer to as a "sensory seeker". He needed tactile input and joint compression. Timothy had a hard time communicating, even with verbal language. Regulating his emotions had been difficult for him. Most of these things were left unaddressed by the school for a long time; a lot of which Julia feels may have played a huge part in him becoming depressed.

Sensory Processing

When Timothy was little and attended EPU, Julia remembers the way he would play with a sensory bin.

Julia said, "We would go in, he was the only kid in there…and he was in the sensory bucket. Not playing with it, not playing outside…he was in the bucket!" They even have a picture of little Timothy in the bucket, "and he's in there…like covered," Julia added.

When he eats, Timothy has always had a tendency to stuff his mouth with food. His mom has to remind him to slow down, even today. When he was little, he would fall asleep with chicken nuggets stuffed in his cheeks.

Trying new foods when he was younger, was quite the challenge. Even now, he'll gag at the site and smell of different foods. It could be something really small, like little pieces of broccoli, and it takes him forever to swallow. Now that he's able to talk and articulate, Julia asks him to explain what the problem is when he's struggling with eating different foods. Julia says he's replied with "mom, I don't know, it's the smell, the texture..I can't.'"

Thinking now that Timothy has a *sensory processing disorder (SPD)*, and must have had it all these years, Julia did what she's always done. She made an appointment for Timothy with his doctor. The doctor agreed that he likely had an SPD. When the doctor asked Julia if she wanted him to make a referral for Timothy to be evaluated, she hesitated for a minute. Then she declined. She said, "I think we'll just live with it." I mean, they had managed through it now for fifteen years and in a sense, Julia had bigger battles to focus on. Plus, Julia pointed out that he's done pretty well with that, without professional help.

Tags on Clothing

When Timothy's was younger, Julia would remove the tags from his clothing. They would bother him. He tries to remove the tags himself now. A few years ago, she bought him a brand new sweater to wear for Christmas. She had him try it on, and complimented him on how nice he looked in it. Julia then told Timothy to take it off, and go put it away in his room. On

Christmas day, Timothy came out of his room without the sweater on. Julia asked about it, so he went back to his room to put it on. When he came out of the room again, she could see there was a big hole in the sweater. "What happened?" Julia asked him. Timothy told her that he ripped off the tag. Feeling a little frustrated at the situation, she realized she has to thoroughly explain what he needs to do. Julia explained to Timothy that if he wants a tag off, he needs to ask her to remove it, not to rip it off himself.

Tactile and Joint Compression: Hop Like a Frog

Looking back to when Timothy was in preschool, Julia says he would get down on all fours and hop like a frog. The teacher at school had told her one time, that no other kids could do that in the class. Timothy's peers would try, but they were unsuccessful. Julia's mom would stress that she shouldn't let him hop anymore, because he was developing worts on his hands from always having them on the ground. So to please her mom, Julia tried to stop the behavior.

One day, when the kids were standing in line at school, Timothy started hopping again, and Julia was trying to stop him. The teacher noticed this. The SDC teacher asked Julia, "why?why can't he do it?" Julia then shared some of her concerns regarding Timothy's hopping behavior with the teacher. Julia remembers the teacher saying, "Okay he has worts…take care of it, but why can't he? If that's what he needs…that sensory input, that joint compression, why can't he do it? Let him." If she let Timothy hop as much as he wanted, Julia was concerned that he could get hurt. Also, she had her mom insisting that she make that behavior stop!

With everything the teacher told her, Julia was now convinced that Timothy's behavior wasn't a bad thing. She just needed to find a way to allow him to do it safely. Timothy would hop into the parking lot. He would also hop in stores, getting in the way of other shoppers and their shopping carts. They couldn't have that.

The teacher helped Julia come up with ways to shape Timothy's hopping behavior. For example, *first,* Timothy would have to walk through the parking lot with his mom, *then,* he could hop on the sidewalk. To avoid him getting in the way, or hit by a shopping cart at the store, Timothy would *first,* walk through the main aisles, *then,* be allowed to hop down the other aisles. "*First* walk - *then* hop", became a readily used tool for Timothy. It made a world of difference in shaping the behavior and teaching him when it was, and wasn't okay to do so. Julia learned an effective way to help her son. Letting Timothy get that joint compression in with hoping using the first-then schedule, "that was a saving grace for me," Julia said.

First-then schedules, are common for teaching kids with autism, an order in which things are expected to happen. It helps with executive functioning, according to, Chicago ABA Therapy (2020). These schedules provide an order in which tasks need to be completed.

Timothy had many odd behaviors. Adopting tools to help shape those behaviors to more appropriate ones, was quite a task for Julia. Sometimes she would get strange stares from others while they were working with Timothy on those behaviors. Julia would have to learn how to advocate for her son, not only in school, but in the community as well.

The Eyes of Judgment

One day, Julia went to pick up her son from school. She arrived a little earlier than usual. There was a grandmother of another student there waiting for dismissal. Julia asked her who she was there for, and she gave Julia the child's name. The grandma proceeded to ask the same of Julia. "I'm here for my son Timothy," Julia Said. "Ooooh — Timothy," the grandma said in a smug tone, as Julia recalls. Julia already had an idea of what this woman was thinking about her son. She wanted to shout out, "you don't know what he's going through, you don't know what's going on in his mind!" Instead she said, "he's just going through some issues, but we're working on it." The grandma responded again with a judging, "oooh — yeah, okay," Julia said.

Remembering that, Julia tells her parents not to judge those kids they hear about doing "bad" or "strange" things often, because they have no idea what the kid is going through. They have no idea what those parents are going through. Sometimes it could be the simplest thing you provide a child, that satisfies a need and extinguishes any negative behavior. It makes it difficult to find those sometimes subtle solutions if you've already made a judgment about that child.

Becoming The Teacher She Needed

From Julia's perspective, she feels that society encourages us to stop behaviors that look "odd". Others encouraged her at one time, to stop her son's hopping behavior, not knowing that it was actually helping him. Timothy was getting physical input that he needed form the hopping. If she listened to what some other people said at that time, he wouldn't have gotten what his body needed. That could've manifested in another more problematic behavior. Today, Julia draws from her experience with Timothy in her own line of work.

Thinking Outside the Box: Sounds Familiar

Julia recalls there being a student in another classroom who was trying to ram into everything. Right away she knew, something other than meets they eye could be going on with this kid. She thought that he very likely *needed* that crashing type of physical input, and quickly came up with a solution to offer the teacher.

Often, both teachers and parents, find themselves looking for ways to stop undesired behaviors entirely. It's obvious we all want to prevent any harmful behaviors from happening. However, as she learned before, if the child's body demanded physical input, strange behavior can arise. To force the child to stop the behavior, could be counterproductive. Instead, she remembered what she had to do with her own son. She gave him an opportunity to continue the behavior (hopping like a frog) in a safe and structured way. It was a win-win! It's especially important for individuals working with Autistic children to remember to shape the behavior, rather than automatically extinguishing it. All behavior serves some purpose, and it's a matter of allowing the child to get what their body needs safely. It's our job (the adults) to uncover exactly what those needs are, in my opinion.

Through her journey with autism, Julia has become aware of the "triggers" for certain behaviors in students. As opposed to when Timothy was struggling with behaviors when he was in elementary school, now Julia has resources at her fingertips. She is in a position, where tools are first handedly available to help support students with disruptive behaviors.

For instance, she explained, at the school where she works, they have sensory balance balls that kids can sit on. Students use them when they have a hard time sitting in a regular student chair. Regarding the child who kept ramming into everything, Julia thought the sensory ball and other things could be useful.

She suggested to the teacher, "let him put his whole body on it, let him crash into the fence, it's okay, he's not gonna get hurt!" She also told that teacher, "have him push the wall, have him do things, don't just say he's the bad kid…"

This student reminded Julia of her own son when he was little. Timothy was labeled "the bad kid", before they really knew everything that was going on with him, and what triggered his maladaptive behaviors. Learning what things influenced Timothy's behavior, was the first step in helping him. The next step, was learning how to help him get through those behaviors. This is something that she's now able to help other students with as a teacher.

Shots Are Painful!

There are some things, no matter how hard you work on them, that remain uncomfortable, with unpleasant reactions or behaviors, if you will. I believe, we have to be comfortable with the uncomfortable.

One of those things for Timothy, are his feelings regarding shots. He does not like them. They are extremely painful to him.

In the seventh grade, Timothy had to get shots. Julia said, "he yelled bloody murder, and said that I was killing him!" Getting shots for Timothy has always been a painful experience for him, according to what he's shared with his mom. Kids with autism and sensory differences, often experience things like pain or touch, in a more heightened way than the rest of us. It's incredibly difficult when others don't understand this.

Timothy looks like any other kid to the outside observer, even with a tremendous amount of stuff going on inside. Julia said, "so I'm here, I'm embarrassed… and everyone is looking at me like, 'what is wrong with him?' I'm like, no no no, you don't understand! There's something going on with him. Yeah he was not diagnosed with PDD, but he has all these other things." Julia remembered thinking all of this, as the other parents in the doctor's office were staring.

She explained, "It was hard to be in it, and it was hard to do it." As she remembers that moment, she was flooded with emotion. "It was hard to be in it because nobody understood him," she said. Julia was stuck between a rock and hard place. She couldn't make everyone understand what was going on with her son in an instant. At the same time, she couldn't make Timothy understand that the need to get the shot, outweighed his discomfort. "I'm yelling at him, and I'm being impatient with him, because..you have to do this," Julia said.

The shot was required by his school. When she came home from the doctor's office that day, Julia told her husband, "you're taking him next time!" It was an extremely stressful situation for everyone involved.

Julia said, "I hated having to do that to him." Her words resonated with me immensely. As a special-needs mom, there are many times that those words describe the situation at hand. Our kids are often plagued with hypersensitivities. We ourselves wouldn't manage those hypersensitivities, as well as they do half the time.

I think these situations are part of what makes us stronger in raising children with autism specifically. Julia feels like those are the moments where you really recognize, that other people *don't* understand what's going on.

Dinosaurs and Other Favorites

When Timothy was little he was obsessed with dinosaurs. That was his thing!

Timothy had a favorite dinosaur. He would always carry it around with him. She had put up a little mock preschool at home for Timothy, since she was going to school to be a teacher at the time. The space was filled with learning materials, like shapes, colors and the alphabet on the wall. She said, "nothing interested him — only dinosaurs!"

After his fixation with dinosaurs, he started taking a real liking to horses. He watched a movie about a horse, over and over again. They bought him a little toy horse figurine that he had to have everywhere with him. Julia explained that Timothy would take that horse to the bathroom, in the bath, to the store and to sleep with him. After his obsession with horses started to disappear, "it was farm animals. It was always animals," Julia said.

He started getting into Transformers in the same way. When this happened, Julia was happy that Timothy was gonna like something that other little boys liked. It was a "typical" thing. Nonetheless, even after his focus shifted to something new, he'd always go back to dinosaurs.

Today, Timothy loves watching youtube, and he puts up videos on his own channel; which are videos of him playing a game…with dinosaurs. The game is pretty simple, and perhaps not very interesting to some people, Julia explained. She said, "they walk around, and have to stay alive, as a dinosaur."

For a long time, Julia wondered when her son's obsession with dinosaurs was going to go away, but now, "I love it," she says. Even now, he'll pick out a t-shirt with a dinosaur on it to wear. Today, it's just one of those things he "nerds out" on, and that's considered "socially acceptable". The only time it gets just a little problematic, is when he wants to go out somewhere in his childhood favorite dinosaur pajamas, now that he's fifteen years old. In fact, Julia shared, "he was gonna go out today… in his pajamas..dinosaur pajamas." She said to him, "Timothy — Pa," trying to get his full attention. She continued, "no Pa. You can't go out in your green high-water dinosaur pajamas, Pa." So Timothy changed into something more appropriate for the outing. We couldn't help but giggle about that just a little bit.

Raising children with special needs makes for unique experiences all the way around. Sometimes you have to laugh, or you might cry. Sometimes things we find silly, might seem incredibly strange, or even absurd to outsiders. The people who are around and supporting us in our lives with special needs, they "get it", and sometimes that's all that matters!

Julia's Support

Gilbert, Julia's husband, has been her greatest support. She can see, just as I can, the impact parenting

special-needs children has on marriages. There have
been plenty of times where they don't see eye to eye, and
yet they find a balance together. Gilbert has helped Julia
calm down in situations where she feels like the world is
spinning out of control. "We've been each other's back
bone, for sure," she added. Gilbert has played a huge
role in assuring Julia that Timothy is who *he is*, and that
it's okay. The new perspective her husband has helped
her develop regarding their son, is different than what
Julia's idea about people with disabilities was, before
their son was born.

Perspective Shift

Growing up, Julia remembers it being a normal
thing for family and friends to fear people who were
different. In the classroom, kids with differences were
often pushed aside even by the educators. This
perspective shaped Julia's point of view, into the early
years of navigating a life with special needs.

"The impact that Timothy has made in people's
lives is so amazing," Julia said with tears welling up.

"My mom, and even my aunt, where they would think something's wrong with him, or something's wrong with you — you did something to cause this," she explained with tears rolling down, "now they can go to a store, and they can say, 'mija, I saw this little boy, and he was having a hard time, and I think he has autism,'" Julia said.

Maybe the kid doesn't have autism, but the point is, they are now more open-minded, and considerate regarding people with differences. Timothy has taught them all to be compassionate and nonjudgmental in his fifteen years on this planet. They've all become more sensitive as well. "He's brought so much awareness to our lives," Julia added.

An Unlikely Advocate

Julia has a brother who she said was in prison at one time. He had an assignment of doing a presentation on a topic that affects society. The assignment made for a great opportunity to learn about something that hit close to home. He chose autism for the topic. Julia said that he took a pamphlet, and learned everything he could on the subject. Because of Timothy, Julia's brother, even though not in the most ideal circumstance, learned a little bit about autism, and shared within his "non-ideal"community. He didn't know anything about autism before, but he loved his nephew, and knew that the impact of this condition was real.

Mrs. Julia

Julia is passionate about teaching educators, the importance of inclusion and mainstream in the schools. She advocates for her *special day class (SDC)* students who have a different way of learning. She lets parents know as soon as she meets them, that her classroom is a mainstream program. She informs parents that their children are going to be exposed to kids that learn differently and have disabilities. She lets parents know that other children don't know how to control there bodies yet, and that's something they'll be working on throughout the school year. While those students are learning how to behave appropriately, their non-disabled student might get hit, bumped, or scratched.

Julia likes to put everything out on the table, and tells parents to let her know if they're not comfortable, so that alternative arrangements can be made. Before parents make that decision, Julia makes it a point to share her personal experience. She tells parents, they're likely gonna hear the name of a child often. This is the child that gets labeled as the "bad kid". She tells them, "this is the one always getting into trouble," because that child was Timothy. Julia reminds them, saying "don't write that kid off, because they're learning."
Being the very first school year for these kids, where they can learn to normalize inclusivity, Julia urges parents to allow their children to be exposed to the differences in her classroom.

Sibling Impact

Elizabeth is the second eldest of Julia's kids. She's also the one who has a harder time with her brother's conditions. When she was little, she would tie her older brother's shoes for him because he didn't know how to. She would pick up after him. When he would have a meltdown, she wanted to know how to help right away. Elizabeth and Timothy started out going to the same school, Julia explained. They would get off the car for school, and Timothy's shoes would be untied. Julia would remind him that he needed try to tie his shoes, and he would tell his mom that he didn't know how. Elizabeth would jump in and do it herself. Julia never asked her to, she would just take it upon herself to do things for her big brother, that she knew he struggled with. In the rush of their days, it was helpful, and it made things quicker and easier, so Julia didn't stop Elizabeth.

Julia feels like Elizabeth does things to overcompensate for everything. She started to want to do everything *right*, and not give her parents any problems. This tendency in her daughter, reminded Julia of herself, in her relationship with her own brother and parents.

It's now become a bit of a resentment for Elizabeth, Julia shared. She asks why her brother doesn't have the same responsibilities that she does. Julia created responsibility/behavior charts at home for her children. Elizabeth complained to mom, about how her brother's chart seemed easier than her own. She would ask Julia why Timothy got a lot of rewards, claiming that he got more than she did. Julia and her husband, had to take a step back and try to figure some way to make things feel fair, but its' still quite the struggle. How can you manage behaviors resulting from unfair conditions — fairly? The rewards for Timothy had to be what seemed excessive to Elizabeth initially, in order to prevent his negative behaviors. While he learned what was expected of him, and how to behave, the incentives faded somewhat. To his sister, not fully understanding the principles at play, It seemed like Timothy was just getting — a lot more rewards than her.

Also, because Elizabeth sees her brother as capable, it makes it difficult for her to remember that things don't come as easy for him as they do for her.

It takes him more practice, and things have to be pulled out of him; whereas Elizabeth eagerly offers her help. In her view, rewards should be based on the value of actions. Timothy's rewards seem beyond the value of his actions to his sister, Julia explained.

Time spent on meetings and appointments for Timothy, were often questioned by Elizabeth when she was younger. It was something "extra" he got. Almost making it a special thing. Why did he have so many special meetings that mom and dad had to go to? She didn't have meetings like that.

Julia says that they don't always know how to manage it. It's an incredibly difficult thing juggling special needs with more than one child in the mix, I can say that with certainty. Finding balance is a challenge. Sometimes Julia's husband will take their daughter to do something special, just with her. They try to give individual time to all of their children.

"Timothy has a little bit more going on and you have to know that. It's not your fault, but you just have to know that," Julia tells Elizabeth. She's discussed with her daughter, that Timothy will likely always have more going on. She cautions Elizabeth that she'll see her brother on a different path, but assures her that it's okay. Timothy's life has taught Elizabeth some hard lessons from a young age. She's learned that some people need more help to succeed. Elizabeth has been a major support not only to her brother, but to her parents, in caring for Timothy. There is a unique dynamic and bond, that's for sure. Timothy is quite blessed to have someone in his life like Elizabeth, from where I stand.

Moments Worthy of Celebration

In the 2019-2020 school year, Timothy got off of an IEP. This was such a HUGE deal to Julia and her family! No longer requiring an IEP represented all of the hard work both Timothy and his parents put in over the years. Julia is incredibly proud of her son. She remembers a time when she thought "he can't" do things, and now Timothy has proven her wrong.

Timothy was in a school play, and him reading his lines, was unbelievable for Julia. He struggled for so long with reading. Getting him to learn ten sight words at one time, was excruciating for him. His incentive for learning those ten sight words was a fifty-dollar dinosaur that he wanted, because it was that challenging for him. Timothy, who's future was very uncertain to Julia much of his life, has made strides in ways bigger than Julia ever saw possible. Kids on the spectrum tend to surprise us on their developmental journey, in big ways.

If She Could Go Back in Time

If she could go back in time, she would have stopped herself from putting so much pressure on Timothy. She feels bad when she thinks back to a time when she spanked him and maybe shouldn't have. There was a toy he wanted from a second-hand store, and it had a broken leg, so she didn't want to buy it. Timothy had a meltdown when he wasn't able to get that toy. Julia sighed, "It was only a dollar," she said. If she could go back in time to that moment, she wishes she would've thought, "get him the toy, it's only a dollar, and he needs it for right now, it's okay," she said. Julia wasn't gonna get him an expensive toy every time he wanted something, but this was just something that he needed in that moment, she explained. Julia felt that she caused that particular preventable meltdown.

There are plenty of times she can think of, she feels that she got it wrong with Timothy. For example, Julia feels she should've understood him better. She shouldn't have disciplined him the way she did sometimes. Sometimes she should've given him what he wanted, or let him do things he needed to do. Julia is grateful that Timothy's preschool teacher, helped her see what Timothy needed. If not for that, Julia would've surely stopped the hopping behavior, and it would've deprived him of what he needed then.

Teach Me ABA

Julia would've insisted the ABA provider actually show her ABA, and how to use it with Timothy, if she could go back in time. The behavioral technician would read little bits out of a binder, and nothing more, Julia remembers. If she could do it again, she explained, "I would have said show me ABA, show me how!"

Demanding an FBA

Julia says that if she could do it all again, she'd be a lot more patient. She would've done her own *functional behavioral analysis (FBA)*, learning what in the environment caused her son's meltdowns, even if she was the cause. "I think as a mom, you feel you have to be the one to be the savior," Julia said. She feels that sometimes her presence was the trigger for certain behaviors, so she should couldn't be the "savior". With an FBA, it would be easier to be patient, because she would know what the *antecedents* were, which would help her, help her son. It's easy for anyone to get impatient, when you don't really know whats going on.

Help Please: More Patience, Less Anxiety

Asking for help from someone else, is something Julia wishes she would have done more of. "He was my baby, he was mine,…I had to fix it," she added. This is something many mothers can relate to. Aside from being more patient with her son, Julia wishes she would have been more patient with herself.

When parents come to her for help, she tells them, "Don't look to the future right now." Julia urges parents to stay in the moment. In adopting this view in her own life, Julia copes much better now with her own anxiety. "Focus on them right now," Julia says. She encourages parents to focus on where their kids are right now, because then parents will be better able to give their kids what they need in the moment. She also makes it a point to tell parents, they did the right thing in coming to her (the teacher) for help. She likes to discretely throw in some helpful terms during those conversations, that parents can use in their IEP's, to help strengthen their advocacy.

Would She Change Him if She Could?

If Julia had access to a cure to rid her son of his autism and other conditions, would she opt for that? In short, her answer is no. Julia explains that her world has changed because of Timothy in a good way. "Not just our little world, but our whole world…it extends to my family, it extends to my friends..to other families in my preschool class, and it will keep extending," Julia said. She plans to continue telling her story, her journey with Timothy, as long as she's a teacher. She wants to help those families looking for answers and searching for hope.

It's a hard decision when she remembers the hard moments. Julia remembers having a conversation with her cousin that has twin boys on the spectrum, when Julia was feeling overwhelmed with Timothy's situation. She remembers being angry with God at that time. She saw her other little girls going to school, easily making friends and just being happy. Her son, he didn't have friends, he didn't get invited to things like his sister Elizabeth. Even today he doesn't. Julia remembers feeling infuriated. She screamed, "why God, why doesn't anyone like him? He likes babies, he likes animals!" Today, she still prays for a friend for Timothy.

Even still, with all the difficult moments on their journey, if it were an option, she would not give him something to cure his autism.

The Gains

Timothy has brought about a lot of understanding of a different world to his family. They are overjoyed in the little accomplishments. "It made the small things in life really big," Julia said. It's still exciting to her when he has any new development.

Julia explained that Timothy has an extremely hard time remembering things. When they give him three-step instructions for tasks that he needs to do, for example, he'll either remember the first or last thing, but will forget the stuff in between. They use visual charts to help him complete tasks. Just the other day, Timothy remembered to take his medication for his skin, all on his own. Taking the medicine was part of a complex sequence for him. That was a huge accomplishment for Timothy! Him telling his mom that he took his medicine, might have seemed like nothing at all to anyone else, but it was such a huge thing for Julia.

Julia also says that her son has brought so much love into their family. She shared that she and Gilbert have gone through so much with Timothy, and they love each other so much more because of that. It's as if they've become stronger through weathering the storm together. "You become stronger as a person, stronger as a parent, and as an advocate," Julia said.

Reflecting: "If I Would've Known Then, What I Know Now."

When Timothy was going through all the assessments in the early years, the notion that "something's wrong", lingered with Julia. Looking back now, she realizes that nothing was ever "wrong" with her son. He was just different and learned in a different way. "I'm perfect in my own way, the way God made me, he's perfect in his world," Julia said. She continued, "this is who he is! We have to accept that, and it's okay."

Overall, Julia's journey with special needs has taken her through many high and low moments. Her journey has been filled with countless assessments, diagnosis and labels. Julia has taken an unpleasant situation and found the positive in it. A change of perspective can certainly go a long way!

Julia continues helping other parents starting on a similar path. She advocates for children like her son, who are different. Timothy is truly a gift to his family! Despite Timothy's struggles, Julia says, "he's brought a lot of joy to our family."

My Take

In this story, we once again read about the experiences through the early years and beyond, with autism. Timothy did face many challenges. Some of which my family has been fortunate enough not to endure. For example, his depression.

Depression can happen to anyone, even a child! Timothy was in elementary school when he was depressed. It's not common that you'd think of that condition within that age group, but in reading this story, I realize the magnitude of the importance of recognizing it. Autism is a neurological condition, and just because you have it, doesn't mean you're exempt from other conditions.

Another important take-away for me, was how Julia leaned on her husband for support. I'm sure there must have been times when tension was thick, but they've been excellent parents, and have learned to recognize the needs of all of their children, together. I can appreciate this having a large family. This leads to an important point. As Julia had discussed with Elizabeth, sometimes the siblings with special needs are going to require extra…everything! Their siblings have to learn to be okay with that.

This story also presents another very important message. When Julia compared her son to her nephew and her cousin, it was helpful to an extent. This was when she was searching for answers to explain Timothy's differences. Then, it backfired, and left her in a position where she was consumed by fear for Timothy's future. I think it's important not to get caught up in comparing your child to other children. I believe that every child is unique, and special in their own light. Every circumstance is different.

Julia is an amazing example of using her experience for a greater purpose. She has pulled from both the positive and challenging times. She's become a better teacher and advocate because of her experience. This story was affirmation for me. It reminded me that my proactive efforts are warranted and necessary. It also inspires me to continue sharing with other families about my experiences, as I find my way through this journey of raising children with autism.

Anchoring Yourself for a Rollercoaster of Experiences Through Autism

The stories presented in this book are incredible, to say the least. I found myself strongly relating to most of these mothers, in at least one area of their journey in raising children with autism. We saw a few similar themes within the different stories.

First, the diagnosis. There was a fight that most of the mothers had to go through, in order to get their children diagnosed and services started. The topic was touched on in each chapter. Then, the educational piece. We heard a bit about the Individualized Education Plan (IEP). Another topic of importance was inclusion. The longing for many of these mothers to have their children included in some way at school, was huge! In chapter 4, Beth talks about inclusion, when Karlee is attending her Christmas program. In Chapter 6, Chelsea had to create a Christmas program for her daughter's class, allowing them to participate in the festivities. In Chapter 9, Julia emphasized the importance of inclusion within her own preschool classroom. Inclusion, is a key element of acceptance.

A message that cried out to me, is how doctors where dismissive of so many of these mothers, when seeking help for their children initially. It is beyond me to know that this is a very real reality for many families. We're taught to look to the pediatricians as the experts to turn to, when any concerns arise regarding our young children. In recent years, it seems as though more practitioners are aware of the signs of autism. Still, there are too many young children with the condition, that fall through the cracks, for lack of recognizing those symptoms early on, in my opinion. I have learned that early intervention is incredibly helpful to overcome the challenges that autism can present. If the symptoms are dismissed by the medical community, then chances are, the child won't receive early intention services. I believe we need to continue to advocate in those areas, for awareness.

A lesson that came up several times, was how these mothers followed their gut instincts. It sounds simple, but if you really think about it, often this meant opposing professional opinions, and even that of family. In Chapter 6, Chelsea followed her instincts, even when her husband wasn't completely on board with having their daughter assessed. In Chapter 2, Claire stood her ground, despite everyone thinking she was wrong. I mean, it's stressful enough when you don't have answers for what's happening with your child. Then, add other's doubting that you know what's best. That can cause unwanted frustration!

We read about both married mothers and single ones. The dynamics differ tremendously between the two in some areas, but the need for support remains the same. Getting your network of support established is essential for success. These women all discussed the tole the rollercoaster of events took on them, what coping strategies they employed, and continue to build upon.

One of the greatest messages for me, was how grounded in faith most of these women are. Their strength resonates in their perception. It is awe inspiring to me. I can relate to the importance of maintaining my faith in God, especially during the most trying of times. I don't know how I'd manage a life with autism, any other way!

In conducting these interviews, I anticipated learning some of the details of the individual stories shared. I wanted to give these incredible women a platform to comfortably disclose their experience in raising children with autism. I was focused on supporting them while they allowed themselves to be vulnerable, and share things that evoked deep rooted emotions. This book was created with all of the readers in mind. I was not planning on what transpired for me in writing this.

Writing this book allowed me to have a unique experience altogether. I was given the opportunity to walk in the shoes of each one of these mothers, through the descriptions and memories they shared with me. I cried when they cried, and laughed when they laughed. I felt the sadness of the battles lost, and cheered for those won. This experience has been an emotional rollercoaster for me. It was for them as well, as they relived each experience.

I want to thank these incredible mothers once again; Jodie, Claire, Carolyn, Beth, Bernadette, Chelsea, Stacee, Paula, and Julia. These nine women, continue to forge forward as autism mothers. I am immensely grateful to have had the privilege to tell their stories.

Glossary

A

Adult Transition Program (ATP) - A program for individuals with disabilities usually between the ages of eighteen and twenty-two years old, which prepares them as best as possible for success as an adult.

Antecedent - Something that happens before a behavior occurs.

Antivaxer - Someone who is opposed to receiving immunizations.

Applied Behavior Analysis (ABA) - A therapy common in the treatment of autism, which focuses on improving behaviors, communication, learning, functional skills, and more.

Asperger Syndrome - A form of autism where language is usually present.

Assistive Technology (AT) - Use of technology, usually an iPad, to assist limited communicators in communicating effectively.

Attention Deficit Hyper-Activity Disorder (ADHD) - A clinical disorder. ADHD makes it difficult for individuals to focus on one thing, and frequently co-occurs with autism spectrum disorder.

Augmentative & Alternative Communication (AAC) Device - Tools and devices used to help individuals that require an alternative mode of communication.

Autism Spectrum Disorder(ASD) - A neurological disorder characterized by challenges in communication, social understanding/interaction, and repetitive/stereotypic behaviors.

Autistic Like Behavior (ALB)Classroom - Classrooms designed specifically for children with Autistic traits.

B

Bilirubin - The yellowish substance that causes jaundice in infants.

C

Candida - A condition characterized by an overgrowth of yeast in the human body.

CBD Oil tincture - an alternative natural medicine used to treat aggression and anxiety for some individuals with autism.

Central Valley Regional Center (CVRC) - An agency which provides some services to clients with special needs, and is responsible for connecting their clients with service providers, and resources in the community.

Chelation - A detoxification process, removing toxins from the human body.

Chemotherapy - A therapy that involves radiation used to treat certain cancers and tumors.

Child Protective Services (CPS) - An agency that is responsible for monitoring the wellbeing of minors.

Comprehensive Youth Services (CYS) - An agency that provides a variety of services such as mediation and counseling for the youth.

Consultation Model - This is a model of collaboration between caregivers and therapists, to carry out therapy for children receiving ABA therapy usually.

D

Disruptive Behavior Disorder - A condition characterized by uncooperative and defiant behavior.

Down Syndrome - A disability marked by extra genetic material from the 21st chromosome.

Due Process - A legal process to resolve a matter in education after other measures have been exhausted.

E

Echolalia - The repeating of spoken words or scripts from television, witnessed in some children with autism.

Electroencephalogram (EEG) - A test to measure brain waves done by use of electrodes placed on the scalp, which measure neurological activity.

Eloping/Eloper - Children that have the tendency to leave suddenly, often running off from where they are without any warning.

Encephalitis - A condition resulting in inflammation of the brain.

Exceptional Parents Unlimited(EPU) - An agency focused on early intervention, testing, and referrals.

F

Fetal Magnetic Resonance Imaging (MRI) - Using strong magnetic fields to take detailed images of organs and tissue of the body, specifically used for imaging of a fetus in the womb.

Fibromyalgia - A medical condition that causes extreme musculoskeletal pain during flare ups.

Flapping - A stimulatory behavior seen in individuals with autism.

Functional Behavior Analysis (FBA) - Data taken through observation to help determine the function of a behavior/(s)

G

Gestational Diabetes - A type of diabetes that develops during pregnancy in some women.

Gastrostomy Tubes (G-Tube) - A feeding tube that is medically inserted in the abdomen as an alternative to oral consumption of food.

H

Hashimotos - A medical condition where the immune system attacks the thyroid area.

Helicopter Parenting - A term used to describe parents who hover over their children, and are somewhat over protective of them.

High Functioning - A term used to describe those individuals with autism who are less severely affected by the condition.

Holistic - a treatment approach that considers all factors that influence a client, such as mental and social factors.

Homeopath - A type of doctor that uses natural approaches to treatments.

Hypertonia - A high level of muscle tone making movements more rigid.

Hyponatremia - A dangerous condition brought about by consuming too much water/fluids.

I

Individualized Educational Plan (IEP) - The legal document that stipulates the types of support a special-education students requires to access their curriculum.

In Home Supportive Services (IHSS) - An agency that employs support workers for individuals with that require support in day to day living.

Individuals with Disabilities Education Act (IDEA) - the legal act which protects the rights of students with several disabilities.

Integrative Medical Clinic - This is a type of medical clinic that may use more than one type of treatment for a patient, such as some traditional and alternative therapies.

Intellectual Disability (ID) - A label given to children with low IQ's and low functional living skills. Previously referred to as "mental retardation".

J

Jaundice - Yellowing of the skin seen in babies. See *bilirubin*.

Jaywalking - Crossing a street where there is no crosswalk. Is considered to be illegal.

L

LAMB - Communication Application.

Level IV Group Home - A type of group home for individuals with severe special needs.

M

Measles, mumps and rubella(MMR) Vaccine - A vaccine given to babies at 12 months of age. This is a vaccine suggested to cause vaccine injury resulting in Autistic-like behaviors, by some antivaxers.

Mental Retardation - See *Intellectual Disability (ID)*

Methylate - A biochemical process, regulating many systems in the human body.

Methylenetetrahydrofolate Reductase (MTHFR) Gene Mutation - A gene mutation changing the way body

systems function, and specifically expel toxins, as it
relates to immunizations.

Mixed Expressive Receptive Language Disorder -
Communication disorder making it difficult to
understand words and sentences.

Mood Disorder - A group of disorders that affects mood
and behavior.

N

Neurotypical - A term used to describe someone without
a disability, who is "normal".

Nonverbal - Without verbal language.

O

Occupational Therapy (OT) - This is the therapy that
focuses on development of skills of the tasks at hand.
Often OT's work with Autistic students on motor skills,
sensory systems, etc., for classroom success, and
functional living.

P

Perseveration - Repetition of a particular response.

Pervasive Developmental Disorder, Not Otherwise Specified (PDD-NOS) - A type of autism diagnosis given to children that have some, but not all the symptoms of the condition.

PICC line - This is formally known as the peripheral inserted central catheter. A flexible catheter used to administer medicine through a peripheral vein.

Picture Exchange Communication System (PECS) - A low tech system used for limited communicators, where pictures are exchanged to express wants and needs initially.

Preverbal - This term refers to nonverbal children, who are believed to have the ability to gain verbal language.

Prologue 2 Go - A communication application

Prompting - Assisting a child to carry out a specific task with full hand over hand help, or partial physical assistance or verbal instruction.

R

Regressed/Regression - When a child looses skills they previously had.

Respite - A break for caregivers where care is provided for the child with special needs.

S

Self-Regulate/Regulation - Finding ways to center the body and emotions, to a calm and comfortable state.

Special Education Local Plan Area (SELPA) - An agency that ensures the rights of special-education students.

Sensory Processing Disorder (SPD) - A condition that makes it difficult to process information through one or more senses.

Sleep Study - Testing done when an individual is asleep, usually overnight at a hospital.

Speech Apraxia - A condition where an individual has difficulty making the accurate movements for speech.

Special Day Class (SDC) - A classroom designed for several students with varying disabilities, ranging from mild to moderate, and moderate to severe.

T

Talk Tablet - A communication application.

Thimerosal - A chemical used in vaccines.

Titers Test - A test that measures antibodies in blood.

Toe Walking - When a child walks on toes or the balls of their feet.

Triennial - Similar to an IEP, but taking place every three years to redetermine the educational plan for special-education students.

Bibliography

Centers for Disease Control and Prevention. 2019.
　　"Autism Spectrum Disorder:Data & Statistics."
　　https://www.cdc.gov/ncbddd/autism/data.html

Chicago ABA Therapy. 2019. "First, Then: Schedules
　　within an ABA Treatment Plan."
　　https://chicagoabatherapy.com/articles/first-then
　　schedules-within-an-aba-treatment-plan

Diament, Michelle. 2010. *"House to Vote on Replacing
　　Mental Retardation with Intellectual
　　Disability."*Disability Scoop.
　　https://www.disabilityscoop.com/2010/09/21/
　　house-rosas-law/10299

Illinois Department of Public Health. 2020. *"Thimerosal and Vaccines."* https://www.dph.illinois.gov/ topics-services/prevenion-wellness/ immunization/thimerosal-vaccines-q-a

Mandal, Ananya, and Robertson, Sally. 2019. *"Chelation Therapy Medical Use."* News Medical Life Science. https://www.google.com/amp/s/ www.news-medical.net/amp/health/Chelation- Therapy-Medical-Use.aspx

Mayo Clinic. 2020. *"Preeclampsia."* https://www.mayoclinic.org/diseases-conditions/ preeclampsia/symptoms/causes/svc-20355745

Medline Plus: Trusted Health Information for You. 2020. *"Newborn Jaundice."* https://medlineplus.gov/ ency/article/001559.htm

National Autism Resources. 2020. *"PDD-NOS Signs, Symptoms and Treatment."* https:// nationalautismresources.com/pdd-nos-signs-symptoms-and-treatment/

National Autism Resources. 2020. *"The Picture Exchange Communication System(PECS)."* https://nationalautismresources.com/the-picture-exchange-communication-system-pecs/

Psychology Today. 2020. *"Applied Behavior Analysis."* https://www.psychologytoday.com/us/therapy-types/applied-behavior-analysis

Rudy, Lisa Jo. 2020. *"Why Your Child With Autism Echoes Words and Sounds."* Very Well health. https://www.verywellhealth.com/why-does-my-child-with-autism-repeat-words-and-phrases-260144

Srivastava, Anand K, and Schwartz, Charles E. 2014. *"Intellectual disability and autism spectrum disorder: Causal genes and molecular mechanisms."* Neuroscience and biobehavioral reviews. https://pubmed.ncbi.nlm.nih.gov/24709068

Index

The Author

The author, Stephanie Ortega-Ramirez, was born in 1982. She is a mother of six children, two of which are diagnosed with autism spectrum disorder (ASD). Stephanie possesses degrees in the fields of Child Development and Psychology, as well as a Master's Degree and PPS Credential, in the field of Counseling and Student Services. Stephanie is PRT (Pivotal Response Treatment) certified, and completed the Project ImPACT (Improving Parents as Communication Teachers). In 2011, with the help of two other mothers, Stephanie founded the nonprofit organization, Fresno Autism Network (FAN). FAN is dedicated to providing supportive services to ASD families in the Central Valley. Stephanie is the author & illustrator of two educational children's books, Only Different: I'm A Kid with Autism, and Mikey's Great Idea: Faith the Size of 10 Pumpkin Seeds. These can be found @ amazon.com. With her education and personal experience with autism,

Stephanie appreciates and highly values, support services for autism geared toward family inclusion. She's also an advocate for autism awareness and acceptance. Stephanie hopes to help autism families learn more about the condition, find support, and intervention approaches that best fit their needs. You can follow her blog, Speaking in My Dreams: A Mother's Experience in Raising Autism, at WorPress.com. Or, for podcast lovers, checkout, The Half of it Podcast with/Steph, available on most major podcast applications.

www.ingramcontent.com/pod-product-compliance
Lightning Source LLC
Chambersburg PA
CBHW062359090426
42740CB00010B/1334